THE ESSENTIAL HABITS OF 6-FIGURE BLOGGERS

Secrets of 17 Successful Bloggers You Can Use to Build a Six-Figure Online Business

Sally Miller

FREE BONUS

As a thank you for buying our book, we have created a bonus area to help you on your journey. The bonus area has a growing list of resources that will help you:

> Finally stop dreaming and start earning money doing what you love.
> Discover proven strategies to build your six-figure online business.
> Get a step-by-step guide that shows you exactly how to build a six-figure blog.

Download your bonus resources at: BloggerHabits.com

Disclaimer

Some of the links in this book may be affiliate links. If you click them and decide to buy something, we may be paid a commission. This won't cost you any extra. We only include links to products or services that we either use or would happily use ourselves.

CONTENTS

INTRODUCTION

I n 2017, Ramsay of Blog Tyrant surveyed 350 bloggers. He found that just eight percent of people interviewed were making more than $10,000 from their blog. Of the remaining 92 percent, the majority (69 percent of people interviewed) were earning zero.

Another survey by ConvertKit revealed a similar picture. Their survey reported that 15 percent of bloggers earned more money than the median United States household income. Whereas, the average profit for the remaining 85 percent was $9,497.

| *The message is clear. Most bloggers don't make a living from their blog.*

Yet, some earn six- or even seven-figure incomes. Online entrepreneurs like Pat Flynn of Smart Passive Income and Michelle Schroeder-Gardner of Making Sense of Cents (who is featured in this book) regularly report six-figure months.

Which leads to an important question. Why do some bloggers earn six figures, yet most do not? What strategies, habits, or systems have led to their success?

To answer these questions, I studied bloggers across various niches. I examined their business strategies. I looked for common themes. I researched their backgrounds, habits, and characteristics.

And while some ideas kept reappearing, I couldn't find a single blueprint for success. Each person followed a unique path.

Of course, this isn't surprising. If success was the result of following a simple formula, then we'd all achieve everything we set our minds to. But this isn't the case.

I persisted. I'm stubborn that way. When I get an idea, I can't let it go. And I was convinced a formula for success did exist. Not only in the blogging world, but in every discipline.

I turned to books like the 7 *Habits of Highly Effective People* and *The Success Principles*. These books helped, and I recommend you read them. They both lay out the common principles of success. However, there was still a problem. Few top performers practiced *all* the ideas in these books.

Then I noticed something interesting. Some ideas were interchangeable and they led to identical outcomes. I started to organize habits and principles into groups. Then I combined groups. I moved things around. I was working toward a framework for success.

Eventually, three types of success habits emerged. At that point, I knew I was on to something. This was a concept everyone needed to know. But first I had to test out my theory. I wanted to be sure the three habits worked.

I returned to the blogging world. Online business was an obvious place to start. Due to the low barriers to entry, there are many examples of successful bloggers— and many more examples of failed ones.

I interviewed 17 successful bloggers. Then I reviewed their answers and cross-checked them against the three habits. An exciting picture emerged: All the bloggers I met *did* practice the three habits.

WHAT TO EXPECT FROM THIS BOOK

This book is a collection of real-life stories. It's also a success manual for bloggers. It captures the accounts of people who have overcome the challenges of blogging and built their dream business.

The people in this book openly share their fears and struggles. They explain what worked for them and what didn't. They hold nothing back. In these pages, you'll discover that building a six-figure blog is not easy. It takes knowledge and determination. Each person I interviewed has a unique business, one that fits them and their vision.

You'll discover the tactics and strategies of successful bloggers. You'll also find that there's no one magic bullet that guarantees success. While some people offer a personalized service, others make money through advertising or affiliate sales. One blogger may swear by product creation. Another will tell you sponsored posts and advertising are the fastest path to success. While most of the people in this book acknowledge the importance of an engaged email list, their opinions on social media differ. Some say it's a waste of time. Others built their blogs by leveraging Pinterest traffic.

> *What are you to do with all this information? Well, here's the good news. Every blogger in this book practices the three success habits.*

These habits are not about specific tactics (though we will cover these). They go deeper. In fact, you can apply these three habits to anything. Not just blogging. Want to lose weight? Pay off your debt? Build a retirement fund? Run a marathon?

> *Practice the three habits and you can do all these things.*

The ideas in these pages aren't new. Instead, this book provides a framework so that you can sort through the mass of information, tools, and techniques and create your own version of success. You'll learn the three habits and how to apply them to your blog, or any other situation.

There are thousands of ways to apply each habit. Success for you won't look the same as it does for me or anyone else. The key is to master each of the three habits by leveraging your unique strengths, experience, and values. This book will give you the steps to do exactly that.

> *By reading this book you will learn from successful bloggers, master the three success habits, and create a six-figure blog that leverages your unique talents and values.*

The rest of this book is divided into three sections, one for each habit. In each part, you will learn how successful bloggers apply the habit and the specific action steps you can take to build your six-figure blog.

But first you need to understand the three habits and how they fit together.

HABIT 1: ACT WITH PURPOSE

The first habit is *Act With Purpose*. Here's what it means:

> *Successful people have a mission and take strategic action to fulfill their vision.*

This habit is about setting meaningful goals and creating a plan to achieve them. It's about being strategic.

I first learned about strategic planning in my corporate job. I worked 18 years for financial institutions like Merrill Lynch, Barclays, BlackRock, and Silicon Valley Bank.

These organizations have a company mission and strategic plan. Each layer of management is responsible for furthering the company mission. New projects or activities must fit the organization's overall vision. This is how complex businesses stay true to their purpose and achieve their end goals.

Now, you don't need to be a large organization to adopt a strategic plan. You can define your mission and set meaningful goals. Then, when you know where you want to go, you can create a plan to achieve your goal(s).

Acting with purpose means you know where you want to go and have a proven plan to get there.

It's important to set goals that align with your strengths and values. This is what is meant by meaningful goals. Once you have your goal, you then implement a strategy to fulfill it. We discuss how to set goals and create a plan for your blog in the next chapter.

Of course, creating an effective strategy takes experimentation. Few people hit it out of the ballpark on their first attempt. Which is one reason why the second habit is important.

HABIT 2: CREATE SYSTEMS FOR SUCCESS

You can have a solid strategy and still fail. You can take courses, learn from experts in your field, and map out a path to success, but fail to meet your goals. Maybe life gets in the way or you don't see results fast enough. This is when many of us throw in the towel.

However, successful people don't give up. They keep going in the face of obstacles. And here's their secret: They don't rely on willpower alone. Here's the definition of habit two:

Successful people create systems so that essential tasks always get done.

Systems are not limited to the computer or software kind. They include daily rituals, outsourcing certain tasks if necessary, content planning, batching related tasks, and more. A system is anything that automates strategic activities.

In section two of this book, we will discuss the systems used by six-figure bloggers. You don't need to adopt all these strategies. In fact, doing so would be overwhelming and almost certainly lead to failure. Instead, select the systems that fit you and your goals.

The bottom line is this:

> *Unless you're superhuman, you need systems to stay consistent and succeed. Don't rely on willpower alone to achieve your goals.*

HABIT 3: BELIEVE IN YOURSELF

Thanks to my corporate career, I had a head start with habits one and two. I have plenty of experience implementing strategies and systems. Yet, for the longest time, I wasn't seeing the results I wanted in my business.

This is because I hadn't mastered the third habit. I was letting my beliefs about money, my abilities, and other people's opinions limit my achievements. Here's what habit three means:

> *Successful people accept responsibility for their results and believe in their power to achieve the desired outcome, no matter what happens.*

Habit three differentiates the six-figure bloggers from the hobby bloggers. It's easy to understand, yet difficult to master. However, actively working on this habit will transform your results.

Let's unpack the definition, so you can truly grasp how habit three works. It has three parts:

1. "Successful people accept responsibility for their results" means adopting a no excuses mindset. When something unexpected happens—which it will—you get to decide how to respond. You can blame outside events or you can change what you're doing. Top performers know that they, and they alone, are responsible for their results.

2. Successful people "believe in their power to achieve the desired outcome." We all carry a set of fears and beliefs. Some of our beliefs hold us back. Habit three means not letting negative thoughts and recurring stories limit your achievement. Instead, you must believe in yourself and your mission.

3. Finally, "no matter what happens" means doing it scared. We're all afraid and we all encounter obstacles. To find success you must lean into your fear and keep moving forward, even when faced with seemingly insurmountable setbacks.

Of the three habits, the third is the most overlooked. It's also the hardest to conquer. Many people focus on strategy and tactics. Adopting new tools or following the latest trend. But, strategy and tactics only get you so far.

Fortunately, there are many ways to strengthen your belief. For example: practicing gratitude, saying affirmations, creating a vision board, surrounding yourself with successful people and meditating. In section three of this book, you'll learn more about the mindset tools used by six-figure bloggers.

DO YOU HAVE WHAT IT TAKES?

Now that you know the habits, which of the three do you most need to work on? Do you have a mission and strategy for your blog? Do you need systems to help you follow through? Are your fears holding you back?

Most people benefit from working on all three habits. In fact, this work never ends. What helps you achieve one goal, won't take you to the next level. You must dig deeper, adopt new systems, and overcome fresh obstacles.

Are you ready for your first challenge? Do you have what it takes to build a six- or seven-figure blog? Let's find out.

SECTION ONE

Habit One: Act With Purpose

CHAPTER 1: ACT WITH PURPOSE

Successful people have a mission and take strategic action to fulfill their vision.

The habits are all important. You can't reach your full potential unless you practice all three. However, habit one is where you want to start. Even if you already have a goal and strategy for your blog, I encourage you to read this chapter and the stories that follow. Make sure you have a firm grasp on the first habit before addressing the other two.

Habit one has two elements:

1. You have a personal mission and set goals that fit with your mission.

2. You follow a proven strategy to meet your goals and omit activities that are inconsistent with your mission.

Holly Reisem Hanna is publisher and founder of the award-winning website, The Work at Home Woman. When Holly first started blogging, she hosted a work-at-home forum. While the forum was popular, it was also an administration overhead. It wasn't generating a return on her investment. Holly eventually closed the forum. In her interview with me, Holly said this:

> *The takeaway is, don't hold on to something that isn't working. Let it go and focus on something new or something that is producing the results you want.*

SIGNS YOU NEED TO WORK ON HABIT ONE

Many bloggers start out strong. They know what they want to write about. They have ideas about how to grow their following and make money. But then things go wrong. Perhaps their blog is growing too slowly or they run out of things to say. The first habit helps you avoid this outcome.

Here are some signs you need to work on the first habit.

1. You don't feel excited about your blog.
2. You don't feel connected to your blog's audience.
3. You struggle to find things to write about.
4. You don't enjoy writing for your blog.
5. You don't know what to do to get people to read your blog.
6. You don't know how to make money from your blog.
7. You don't have enough money or time to manage your blog.

If any of these statements ring true for you, then keep reading. In the rest of this chapter, I will show you how to master habit one by getting clear on your blog's purpose and setting a strategy that will help you fulfill your mission. Let's get started.

YOUR BLOG'S PURPOSE

When your goals align with your purpose, the work becomes effortless. For bloggers, this means having a reason why your blog exists—one that is meaningful and unique to you. A reason that goes beyond sharing advice or stories with family and friends.

There's arguably nothing more important than getting clear on your personal mission. Michelle Schroeder-Gardner, founder of Making Sense Of Cents, describes how she learned this lesson.

When starting out, Michelle took on freelancing clients to supplement her blogging income. This is what she told me during our interview:

> *I was stuck working for others and I wasn't passionate about it. Many people love freelancing, but I knew my calling was to grow my blog. And by spending time on client work, I couldn't focus on Making Sense of Cents. This held me and my blogging business back.*

> *So, one day, I decided to "fire" my freelance clients and dedicate 100 percent of my time toward my own business. My income quickly doubled after that, even though I took a big hit by firing my clients!*

Michelle now regularly reports six-figure months and is one of the most financially successful bloggers interviewed for this book. In March 2018, Michelle reported a monthly income of $241,649. After expenses and fees, she earned approximately $231,327.

Having a mission means making your blog about something bigger than yourself. Finding an audience for your blog that you can connect with and want to serve. In the rest of this section, I will walk you through an exercise to help you find your blog's purpose.

There are five steps in the process:

1. Get clear about what matters.
2. Write your mission statement.
3. Write your guiding principles.
4. Set meaningful goals.
5. Review your goals.

STEP 1. GET CLEAR ABOUT WHAT MATTERS

It's time to reflect on your life and what matters most to you. Don't be tempted to rush this exercise. Spend time in self-reflection and dig deep.

Grab your favorite journal or download the Blogger Success Habits Workbook and answer the following questions. You can download the workbook at BloggerHabits.com.

(NOTE: These questions are influenced by Todd Henry's excellent book *Louder Than Words*.)

> *1. When are you at your best? When do others respond most to your ideas? What are your unique strengths?*
>
> *2. When are you moved emotionally? When can you recall getting emotional about something you experienced? Why were you moved?*
>
> *3. What stirs you to compassionate anger? When do you get angry on behalf of someone else who has been wronged?*

> 4. What gives you great hope? When have you taken a position, even in the face of skepticism or criticism from others?
> 5. What kind of problems are you naturally drawn to solving? What are the qualities of the problems you are drawn to?

I suggest you have two or more brainstorming sessions. After the first session, put your answers to one side. Then come back a day later and add any new ideas. This gives your subconscious time to ponder the answers to these questions and for new thoughts to occur to you.

You will be using your answers to these questions to form a purpose for your blog and to set your blogging goals.

STEP 2. WRITE YOUR MISSION STATEMENT

The next step is to write your mission statement. What do you want to create or achieve with your blog? Who will read your blog and how will they benefit? How will your actions change the world (or some part of it)? What do you dream about doing?

Your mission may impact your local community, a distinct group of people, or the entire world. It can't be too big or too small. But it is something that matters deeply to you.

Think of your mission statement as a compass. It's your North Star. In his bestselling book, *The 7 Habits of Highly Effective People*, Stephen Covey's second habit is, "Start with the end in mind." He wrote:

> *How different our lives are when we really know what is deeply important to us, and, keeping that picture in mind, we manage ourselves each day to be and to do what really matters most.*

Review your answers from step one. Look for problems you're drawn to solve, people you're moved to help, positive change you want to see in the world. We all have themes, movements, ideas which ignite us. What moves you?

In your journal or workbook, write a brief mission statement for your blog. Think in terms of who you want to help and what you want to do for them. But don't worry about getting this perfect. One of my favorite mantras is, "Clarity comes from action." Your mission will become clearer as you take steps to fulfill it. Do the best you can right now. You can always refine your mission statement later.

Here're some real-world mission statements to inspire you:

> 1. Headspace: "To improve the health and happiness of the world."
> 2. HEIFER International (non-profit): "To work with communities to end world hunger and poverty and to care for the Earth."
> 3. Microsoft: "To empower every person and every organization on the planet to achieve more."
> 4. Virgin Atlantic Airways: "To embrace the human spirit and let it fly."
> 5. Zappos: "To provide the best customer service possible."

STEP 3. WRITE YOUR GUIDING PRINCIPLES

Now, I want you to create some guiding principles. These are a set of rules or ideas that guide your decisions. Your guiding principles reflect how you want to live. Think of it like this:

> Your mission statement defines who your blog serves and what difference you make in the world. Your guiding principles specify how you fulfill your mission.

It's possible to set goals that align with your mission, but if they aren't also consistent with your values then you'll struggle to stay motivated. Here's an example from my business. In 2017, I ran an online challenge to help people write and publish their book. This was consistent with my mission, but it violated two of my guiding principles:

1. Keep it simple: The challenge had many moving parts and I felt frustrated with the process.

2. Use my talents: I thrive in one-on-one and solitary activities. The large, group environment of a challenge didn't play to my strengths.

During the challenge, I felt drained. It took considerable willpower to show up each day and give it my best. It wasn't sustainable and I didn't want to repeat it. This contrasts with one-on-one coaching and content creation (books, programs, articles, emails). When I'm doing these things, I'm engaged and produce my best work. Motivation isn't a problem.

When are you at your best? What values are most important to you? What are your unique strengths?

Re-read your answers from step one. Look for recurring themes and values. Focus on identifying what matters most to you. Then, distill the themes into five or more guiding principles. This may take some time. Try combining related ideas and eliminate anything that's lower priority.

For example, here're my guiding principles:

1. Use my talents to help people (eliminate or outsource what I'm not good at).
2. Seek the truth (don't chase trends and share untested ideas).
3. Keep it simple (don't overcomplicate).
4. Do my best (don't take shortcuts).
5. Focus on the journey (and not the end result).

STEP 4. SET MEANINGFUL GOALS

Once you have a mission statement and guiding principles, you're ready to define your blog goals. Use whatever goal setting method you like. If you prefer to dream big then define at least one BAHG—Big Audacious Hairy Goal. If you favor SMART goals, then use that methodology.

> Goals matter. They keep you on track and, providing your goals are meaningful, they help you stay motivated.

Brainstorm what you want to achieve with your blog in the next three to twelve months (pick a period that works for you). I favor goals with a specific outcome. For example: publishing a book, launching a product or service, or learning a new skill.

You can have one goal or a handful of goals. I prefer to pursue one major goal at a time. But I may also have one or two smaller goals. Make sure each goal does two things:

1. Your goal should bring you closer to fulfilling your personal mission. You should feel excited about fulfilling your goal.
2. Your goal should be consistent with your guiding principles. Pursuing the goal should not require you to act in a way that's inconsistent with your highest values.

STEP 5. REVIEW YOUR GOALS

Finally, review your goal(s) by answering the following questions:

1. Does each goal align with your mission statement? If not, consider amending or cancelling any goals that don't fit.

2. Does each goal align with your guiding principles? Again, consider amending or cancelling any goals that don't fit.

3. OPTIONAL: If you complete the goals in the desired timeframe, will you meet your financial goals? If not, what else do you need to do?

4. Do you have sufficient resources (time, skills, money) to achieve these goals? If not, do you need to amend or cancel any goals? Do you need to add time or add new goals so you can obtain the necessary skills?

5. If you pursue these goals, will you be living your best possible life?

Once you're satisfied with your mission statement, guiding principles, and goal(s), put them somewhere you can easily refer to. I keep mine on my cell phone and in the front of my journal. This way I can always refer to them on a daily basis.

Congratulations. You now have meaningful goals that align with your mission. Goals that reflect who you are and what matters most to you. You are halfway to mastering habit one. Next, you want to define a strategy for your blog that will take you from where you are now to where you want to be.

YOUR BLOG STRATEGY

There are countless experts online who can show you how to build an income producing blog. This is both good and bad. On the one hand, education is important. You want to learn from people who are already doing what you want to do.

The problem, of course, is that there's too much information. If you attempt to learn everything there is to know about SEO, social media, content marketing, product creation, affiliate marketing, etc., you will spend all your time learning and no time doing. You don't need to implement every tactic or piece of advice to be successful.

Instead, you want to find a handful of activities that work for you and your blog. Then, focus on just those things. If something isn't working for you, be prepared to tweak your strategy or let it go. Keep trying new ideas, testing, and tweaking until you land on the strategy that works for you.

Your blog strategy should have at least three components:

1. A clearly defined purpose and audience. This is your blog's mission statement which you created earlier in this chapter.

2. A monetization strategy.

3. A marketing strategy.

In the rest of this chapter, I will walk you through the most common blog monetization and marketing strategies. But don't try all these methods at once.

> *Do not overcomplicate your blog strategy. Start with one monetization and one marketing strategy. Then build from there.*

It's much easier to see if something is working if you're only implementing one thing at a time. This also allows you to focus your efforts, which greatly increases your chances of success.

As you define your strategy, always put your audience first. Dave Stuart, Jr. of davestuartjr.com, is a full-time high school teacher and father. Finding time to blog was a challenge for him. Yet, by focusing on his readers, Dave has built a six-figure blog and is fulfilling his mission to help other teachers. Here's what Dave told me:

> *Putting images with my blog posts and obsessing over Twitter followers [...] haven't mattered much to my long-term success—writing helpful things has. That's it.*

Later, he added:

> *Write 100 helpful, reader-centric blog posts, as quickly as you can. Fret not about web design. Just make sure you're treating your reader as you'd like to be treated.*

Your blogging strategy doesn't need to be complex. Know who you're writing for and create amazing content for them. The rest will follow.

MONETIZATION STRATEGIES

Below is an overview of the most popular ways to make money from a blog. This list isn't exhaustive, nor is it meant to be a step-by-step guide to monetizing your blog. If you want a more in-depth discussion of each method, you can also read my book *Make Money From Blogging*.

As you read through the options, note one or two strategies that fit your strengths. If you love connecting with people, then you could offer a service. If you prefer creating, then consider product creation. Or if you want to focus on writing amazing blog content, affiliate marketing and advertising might be best for you.

Let's dive in.

MONETIZATION STRATEGY 1: AFFILIATE MARKETING

Affiliate marketing means you are promoting someone else's product or service. When you sign up as an affiliate for a company or brand, you receive an affiliate link. This link has unique identifying characters in it.

Once you have your link, you share the product or service with your audience. When a visitor clicks through your link and makes a purchase, you receive a commission. You can promote your affiliate links in various places:

> Write a blog post reviewing the product.

> Compare and contrast two products.

> Write a round-up of five of the best products.

> Promote the product in a tweet.

> Post a Facebook update about the product.

> Create an appealing pin and link it with your affiliate link.

> Do a Facebook Live about the product and include your affiliate link in the comments.

Before sharing an affiliate link, make sure you're aware of the brand's terms and conditions. For example, some companies don't allow you to share your links via social media.

Also, you must tell your readers that you will benefit from their purchase. In addition to having a full disclosure page on your blog, you need to include a disclosure on every single post that contains an affiliate link.

If you're interested in learning more about affiliate marketing, I recommend Michelle Schroeder-Gardner's course, Making Sense Of Affiliate Marketing. (By the way, that link is my affiliate link!)

MONETIZATION STRATEGY 2: PRODUCT CREATION

Selling your own products is a little more complex than being an affiliate for someone else. However, the potential returns are far greater. You can also create something that's an ideal fit for your blogging audience, thereby serving them at a deeper level.

Here are five common products bloggers create:

1. Ebooks
2. Downloadable products (workbooks, bookmarks, a PDF game, customizable labels, etc.)
3. Courses
4. A video series
5. An audio-based training series

If you want to create a product, spend time getting to know your audience's needs. What are their secret hopes and deepest pain points? What can you create to help them achieve their dreams and overcome their problems?

Blogging success always comes back to one thing. Know your audience and serve them at the deepest level possible.

MONETIZATION STRATEGY 3: OFFERING SERVICES

Providing a service is a fast way to monetize your blog even if you have a small following. Think about what you enjoy doing and what you're good at. What services are people willing to pay for? Then, add a Hire Me or Services page to your website.

Here are ten services you could offer:

1. Freelance writing
2. Virtual assistant work
3. Graphic design
4. Coaching
5. Photography/stock photos
6. Web design
7. Proofreading/editing
8. Social media management
9. Bookkeeping
10. Blog management

Start with one service and tailor it to your audience's needs. Test out your idea by contacting people who might be interested in your service. When I started coaching,

I emailed 119 of my subscribers who had told me they wanted to publish a book. Here's the email I sent:

> *Hi there,*
> *How's your weekend going?*
> *I'm reaching out to see if you're interested in my new coaching program. This is a coaching intensive for aspiring authors who are ready to finally write and publish their book.*
> *Does this sound like you or anyone you know?*
> *If so, please hit reply and I'll send you all the details. The program starts in March and I'm accepting applications up until Friday, March 3rd.*
> *I hope to hear from you soon!*
> *All the best,*
> *Sally*

This short email resulted in my first three paying clients and $1,300 in revenue. At the time, I didn't have a Hire Me page on my website. Keep putting yourself out there. And if your first idea doesn't work, tweak your offering or try something new.

MONETIZATION STRATEGY 4: ADVERTISING

You can earn money by allowing advertisements on your blog. Bloggers have several advertising options open to them. The first is Pay Per Click (PPC). For PPC ads, you earn a small amount each time a reader clicks on the ad. You partner with an ad network and give them space on your site.

Some popular PPC companies are:
> Media.net
> Google AdSense
> Clickbooth
> BlogAds
> Infolinks

If you have decent traffic, you can work directly with companies to sell advertising space. Before approaching a company, you want to have a media kit to share. This includes specific information about your traffic and the demographics of your readers.

Other options include Amazon native shopping ads. These allow you to refer shoppers to Amazon. If they make a purchase, you receive a small commission. These are sort of a hybrid between affiliate marketing and ads.

Affiliate marketing and advertising are the two most passive monetization strategies, though no income source is 100 percent passive. You still need to monitor your traffic and sales to make sure your efforts are paying off.

MONETIZATION STRATEGY 5: SPONSORED POSTS

As a blogger, you can partner with brands to create sponsored posts. These are blog posts a company pays you to write. Often your post will need to include a link to a specific product.

You can find sponsored post opportunities through influencer media networks, by reaching out to brands directly, or through advertising and having brands find you. Some media networks that work with bloggers are:

> Tapinfluence
> Izea
> She Speaks
> Mom it Forward

You may need to meet certain traffic and social media stats before you qualify to join these networks. The more engaged your audience is, the more value you offer the brand.

If you are interested in doing sponsored posts, make sure you have a media kit with information about your demographics, blog stats, and social media following. This gives brands the information they need to decide whether to work with you.

MONETIZATION STRATEGY 6: HOSTING EVENTS

The last monetization option is hosting events. Events range from an hour-long webinar to multi-day online summits. In-person conferences, meetups, and workshops are other possibilities.

The scope, speakers, and attendance of your event each affect your earning potential. A small one-day meetup with your readers won't bring in as much income as a multi-day virtual summit with influencers in your niche.

Hosting a multi-person event is also an excellent way to build connections with other bloggers in your niche. We will discuss collaboration in more detail below.

MARKETING STRATEGIES

You've decided how to monetize your blog. Now, you want people to read your content. The more visitors your blog attracts, the more money you earn and lives you change. However, not all traffic is the same. You want the right visitors to find and read your blog. These are the people you want to serve to fulfill your blog's mission statement.

The Internet is a vast place, and there's no one marketing strategy that will guarantee your success. All the following methods take time before gaining traction. And some work better for different audiences. As always, the key is to find the approach that works for you. Pick one marketing strategy and give it your full attention for several months. If you're not seeing an increase in readership then tweak your strategy or move on to the next.

Monica Froese, blogger at Redefining Mom, says this:

> *Don't be afraid to do things your way. I think a lot of times I see bloggers get stuck in the cycle of chasing the newest trends and it ends up sending them in circles.*

By focusing on her zone of genius, Monica grew her blog to six figures in just 15 months. The lesson is to know yourself and discover what works best for you.

MARKETING STRATEGY 1: SEARCH ENGINE OPTIMIZATION (SEO)

An SEO strategy helps you connect with people who need what you have to offer. It gets the right traffic to your site. Keywords play an important part in SEO. Keywords help people find your blog. They tell Google (and other search engines) what your post is about.

Keywords are simply what people type into search engines while looking for information. They can be short, such as, "dogs," or long, e.g. "how do you housetrain a puppy?"

The longer keyword phrases are more specific. These are called long-tail keywords. As a beginning blogger, you should focus on long-tail keywords. There are many blogs out there. And with all the information available, you want to deliver exactly what people are looking for.

You can find keywords using a tool like KW Finder. Or you can use Pinterest to find potential keywords. Pick a topic and type it into the search bar on Pinterest. As you type, Pinterest suggests keyword phrases based on what you enter. These are all potential long-tail keywords you can plan your post around.

When you write your post, incorporate the keyword into the text (but don't overdo it). You can also use the keyword in the post title, headings, meta description, url, and image alternative text. Incorporating the keyword in these places helps users find your article when they are searching on the Internet.

MARKETING STRATEGY 2: SOCIAL MEDIA

Many of the bloggers interviewed for this book leveraged the power of social media to build a large blogging audience. However, be careful about spending too much time on social media. A large social media following doesn't always translate into more blog readers and a bigger income.

Research the different social media platforms to see where your audience is hanging out, then pick a platform and dive in. No matter which platform you decide to use, here are some tips to help you promote your content.

1. Experiment with post styles to see what type of content your followers engage with.

2. Use your data. See which posts are performing (e.g. by sending readers to your blog) and look for patterns. Find out when your users are active and adjust your posting schedule accordingly.

3. Use scheduling tools to help you schedule posts in bulk. This way you aren't glued to social media all day long.

4. Remember to build relationships. Respond to comments and join the conversation on other people's posts when you can.

MARKETING STRATEGY 3: OTHER PEOPLE'S AUDIENCES

When you connect with other bloggers, you can share your ideas with someone else's audience and then invite them back to your blog. One way to do this is by guest posting. This is when you write a post that someone else publishes on their blog.

You often receive a bio at the end of your guest post and can include a link back to your blog. This way, readers who are interested can click through and find you. It also gives you an external link to your blog, which is beneficial.

While there are huge sites that offer guest posting opportunities (like Money Saving Mom), you may need to start off with smaller blogs. As you gain more experience, you can work your way up to blogs with lots of readers.

Guest posting isn't the only way to leverage someone else's audience. Being interviewed on a podcast is a quick and easy way to connect with new people. You can also collaborate with other bloggers on a new project. We will discuss this option next.

MARKETING STRATEGY 4: COLLABORATION

As you make connections in your niche and the blogging world, you'll discover opportunities to collaborate with others. Collaboration is a wonderful way to support other bloggers and spread your message to each others' audiences.

There are many ways to collaborate. This book is an example. Multiple bloggers contributed to this book and we're all sharing the book with our followers. We are all benefitting from group marketing. You can also take part in an online summit, organize a joint webinar, or write a round-up post in which you link to other bloggers' content and then ask them to share your post.

The key to a successful collaboration is to build relationships with people who have an audience like yours and who share your values. Then work together in a way that benefits everyone. Always think about what the other person gains from the project. Never focus on your own needs. When you enter a relationship thinking about what you can give to someone else, you'll build strong connections much faster. And you will gain a reputation as someone who is worth connecting with.

Christina Scalera, attorney and founder of The Contract Shop, talks about how forming strong connections helped her find success. Here's her advice for new bloggers just starting out:

> *I'd find three people as "mentors" and follow their every move like a fangirl until they noticed me. If they accepted me, I'd create a partnership with them and get in front of their audience, maybe via a newsletter swap or being a guest on their podcast. If they did not accept me, I'd find a new person and rinse/repeat until I found my three. Then I'd leverage the relationships from there. This isn't using people. I've followed this strategy and some of my connections are now my best friends.*

MARKETING STRATEGY 5: PAID ADVERTISING

This last marketing strategy is not recommended for beginners. You only want to pay for advertising once you are successfully monetizing your blog and have a clear picture of who your audience is. If you start doing paid advertising too early, you risk spending thousands of dollars targeting the wrong people and getting zero return on your investment.

Facebook advertising is a popular form of paid advertising for bloggers. Other options include Pinterest advertising, Google Adwords, and YouTube advertising.

In all cases, you must be clear on who you are targeting, what those people want, and how you are going to get a return on your ad expenditure.

MARKETING STRATEGY 6: EMAIL MARKETING

Just about every blogger interviewed for this book emphasized the importance of building an email list. Email marketing is less about building a following and more about forming a relationship with people who have already discovered you.

Most experts agree that your email list is more important than your social media following. Social media networks are always changing their algorithms. The people who follow you might not see the content you share. You don't own the platforms, and you don't have any say in changes that happen.

What you do own, however, is your email list. It's your direct line to your readers. Before you can start collecting email addresses, you'll need to sign up for an email service provider like ConvertKit or MailerLite. You can then add signup forms to your website so that your readers can enter their email address and join your list.

Here's what Terra Dawn, blogger at Uncork Your Dork, says about email marketing:

> For a while, I was super focused on creating downloads and blog posts to increase my list numbers. What I've learned is that it isn't about the list size. It's about how focused that list is.

The key is to attract your ideal followers (and not just anyone) to your website. Then encourage them to join your email list. Finally, nurture your subscribers as if they were your best friends. Here's what Terra went on to say:

> In the beginning, I was so focused on getting those numbers up that I overlooked the people those number represented. They weren't dedicated to my topic and worse yet, they weren't dedicated to me. I've since deleted close to 45 percent of my list, but it's more engaged and active than ever. I make 10 times the sales and get 10 times' the excitement as a response to my weekly newsletters!

ACTION STEPS

If you'd like a guide to all the action steps in this book, download the Blogger Habits Workbook at BloggerHabits.com.

1. Complete the five steps at the beginning of this chapter and define your blog's purpose:
> Step 1: Get clear about what matters.
> Step 2: Write your mission statement.
> Step 3: Write your guiding principles.
> Step 4: Set meaningful goals.
> Step 5: Review your goals.

2. Research the monetization options and decide how you want to make money from your blog. The most common monetization strategies are:

> 1: Affiliate Marketing

> 2: Product Creation

> 3: Offering Services

> 4: Advertising

> 5: Sponsored Posts

> 6: Hosting Events

3. Pick one or two marketing strategies and commit to these for the next three months. At a minimum, make sure you're building an email list. Here're the marketing strategies described above:

> 1: Search Engine Optimization (SEO)

> 2: Social Media

> 3: Other People's Audiences

> 4: Collaboration

> 5: Paid Advertising

> 6: Email Marketing

As you work through these action steps, take time to read the stories in the following chapters. Each blogger I interviewed has mastered habit one and has a successful income-generating blog.

Also study their websites and follow the bloggers who interest you. Can you see their vision? What marketing and monetization strategies are they using? Learn from the people who are already doing what you want to do. This is how you'll create your own successful blog and start making a difference in the world.

CHAPTER 2: MICHELLE SCHROEDER-GARDNER

I knew my calling was to grow my blog.

Michelle Schroeder-Gardner is the founder of Making Sense of Cents, a personal finance website that helps readers learn how to save more, earn money, and live a better life. She earns over $100,000 a month from her blogging business and shows no signs of slowing down. She currently travels full-time with her husband and two dogs via sailboat.

> **How long did it take from starting your blog/online business until you were consistently earning $8,000 per month or more?**

In the summer of 2011, I started Making Sense of Cents with the aim of teaching people how to save money as well as journaling about my personal finance experiences. I had read a magazine that featured a personal finance website in one of their articles. I followed that website and my interest in blogging grew from there. Before that same summer, I had no idea what blogs were or that they could be a source of income.

I did not start my blog with the intention of making money from it. It was a hobby and an outlet. However, I grew to love blogging and now I'm a full-time blogger. I went full-time in October of 2013 and I haven't looked back since. Blogging has changed my life for the better and it's something that I recommend everyone try if they are interested.

Around two years after starting Making Sense of Cents, I was earning $5,000 to $10,000 a month. For the first year it was a hobby and I wasn't trying to make money. It took about one year of focused effort to start earning $8,000 per month or more.

> ## What single strategy or habit had the biggest impact on your business when going from zero to $100,000?

One of the big things I did was focus on my own business. In the beginning, when I first became full-time self-employed, I still worked other people's businesses. I was a freelance writer, social media manager, and more. It paid the bills and helped me leave my soul-sucking day job to work from home full-time.

However, I wasn't happy. I was stuck working for others and I wasn't passionate about it. Many people love freelancing, but I knew my calling was to grow my blog. And, by spending time on client work, I couldn't focus on Making Sense of Cents. This held me and my blogging business back.

So, one day, I decided to "fire" my freelance clients and dedicate 100 percent of my time toward my own business. My income quickly doubled after that, even though I took a big hit by firing my clients!

> ## What new habit or routine has most improved your life in the last year?

I "batch" a lot of my tasks. For example, I'm always at least a month ahead in content. Sometimes, I'm three months ahead. I do this by batching my writing. I write a bunch of content at once, and then take a month or two off to focus on other tasks.

I love writing. But, over the years, I've found that I write best and enjoy it the most when I dedicate a few days or even a week toward writing as much as I can. Once the ideas start flowing, it's hard for me to stop.

> ## When did you hire your first virtual assistant or other help? What advice would you give new bloggers regarding outsourcing?

I've hired help since the beginning, but I didn't hire my first editor and my first virtual assistant until 2017. I used to contract out one-off projects. Now I have an ongoing team who help with my blog. This has saved me so much time and it's nice not to do everything in my blogging business 100 percent of the time.

My top tip for new bloggers is to hire and outsource when you think you need it. By outsourcing, you free up your time to focus on the tasks you do best.

What would you do differently if you were to start a new blog/online business today (and couldn't leverage your existing audience)?

Honestly, I'd not change much. I may try some new strategies, such as attempting a YouTube channel. But, that's only because I've never done that and sometimes it's fun to try something new!

Looking back now, what is something you worried about/spent too much time doing that wasn't important down the road?

I would say that having the wrong mindset wasted a lot of my time in the beginning.

For example, I've always been interested in affiliate marketing. But at first, I didn't think it was a realistic way to make money. I thought you needed a huge following and a ton of page views to be successful with affiliate marketing.

Then, one day, I set a goal to earn some affiliate income. I consistently worked on my goal and soon I was earning a few dollars each month. My earnings grew month after month. My affiliate earnings are now a significant portion of my blogging income. You don't need a lot of page views or a huge following to make a great income through affiliate marketing.

I love affiliate income because it's mostly passive. You create an article or social media post and can earn money from it years down the line. Although you do need to maintain the original posting and keep sending traffic to it. With affiliate marketing, I can earn a great living promoting products that I use and enjoy.

A bad mindset is something that holds people back. Don't let your doubts stop you from trying something new.

What was the biggest obstacle you faced in building your business to where it is today? How did you overcome it?

I don't know if it's the biggest obstacle, but one that's always on my mind is managing a good work-life balance.

As a full-time blogger, taking a break from blogging can be difficult. It's easy to work 24/7, and as your own boss, you know that every minute is an opportunity to improve your business.

Finding a good work-life balance means taking breaks from work to enjoy life. It's important that you aren't glued to a screen 24/7. Enjoy what's going on around you, be present in the moment, and have a life outside of work. Even if you are enjoying your work, a break is good. A bad work-life balance can make you irritable, stressed, impact your relationships, and affect your health.

I've done many things to manage a better work-life balance, such as:
> Working ahead as much as I can
> Taking time off
> Attempting to be "okay" with working building up
> Being more efficient with my time
> Unplugging
> And more!

What's your advice for bloggers who are still struggling?

My best piece of advice is give it a go! I waited so long to try my hand at affiliate marketing, and I regret waiting so long. Even if you have few followers or if you are a brand new blogger, you can still be successful at affiliate marketing.

Another major blogging mistake is not making the effort to network. Networking is so important as a blogger. You should see others in the blogging world as your colleagues and friends, not your enemies or competition.

How can readers connect with you?

You can find me on my personal finance and lifestyle website, MakingSenseOfCents.com. If you want to follow my full-time travels, I recommend following me on Instagram. I also have a great personal finance community that is free on Facebook, a Pinterest account, Twitter, and more!

CHAPTER 3: MONICA FROESE

Listening to my audience and creating products they were asking for has been key to my success.

Monica Froese is a mom, wife, and business strategist for mom entrepreneurs. She has an MBA degree in finance and marketing and blogs at Redefining Mom, a site for helping moms build thriving online businesses. In 2015, she traveled to the White House to discuss family-friendly workplace policies with the President's senior advisors and has been featured on several media outlets including Fox News, Scary Mommy, Healthline, and Mom Talk Radio. With her tactical approach to balancing family and online business, she helps moms build successful businesses and change their lives at the same time.

What is your favorite business book and why?

Profit First by Mike Michalowicz is my favorite business book. First, Mike has a very relatable story and his ability to be vulnerable draws in his audience. Second, coming from a business background in finance, I find his way of looking at balance sheets fascinating. I started implementing his strategies in 2018 and have managed to considerably cut down expenses and pay myself 20 percent more than I did in 2017.

How long did it take from starting your blog/online business until you were consistently earning $8,000 per month or more?

I started Redefining Mom in July of 2013 while I was still working my corporate job in marketing for a Fortune 100 company. I didn't try to monetize my blog until August of 2016. I built a foundation, but had put very little work into monetization prior to this. By February of 2017, I saw income spikes to $10,000 on certain months. By November of 2017, my income was steadily above $10,000 a month. It took roughly 15 months.

What single strategy or habit had the biggest impact on your business when going from zero to $100,000?

For months I was working extremely hard but focusing on low ROI (return on investment) tasks and sometimes tasks that had no ROI at all. I was trying to do everything instead of honing in on my area of genius. By listening to my audience, it became clear they wanted something specific from me. They wanted me to teach them how to read and understand analytics and use that information to make informed decisions on about how to structure their sales funnels. Listening to my audience and creating products they were asking for has been key to my success.

The other thing I'll say is I've always treated my blog as a business. I keep regular work hours and even though my schedule had to shift while I was pregnant for the last half of 2017 and early 2018, I still made sure work time was work time and family time was family time. I see many people try to build blogging empires while they are also the sole caregiver. I think that's extremely hard to do when your attention is always split at any given time.

What new habit or routine has most improved your life in the last year?

I loathe working out, but I know it's an important part to my mental and physical health. I found a local gym that offers HIIT (high intensity interval training) for one-hour sessions. They have an app so you can book your session ahead of time. I've found that scheduling my workout first thing in the morning helps me feel accomplished, and I have much more mental clarity when I sit down to work. I'm way more productive now that I've added these workouts into my daily routine.

When did you hire your first virtual assistant or other help? What advice would you give new bloggers regarding outsourcing?

Outsourcing is one of the hardest things I've done in my business. I'm a self-proclaimed control freak. Almost two years ago, I had a reader reach out to me and let me know she followed my free blogging guide to start her own business. We quickly became good friends and she's now one of my best friends. She was my first hire because I trusted her. I knew she understood my business. As she and I have continued to grow, I've had to look into building a sustainable team. I've recently hired a new VA who is super detail oriented and someone I trust to anticipate my needs and pitch in where I need her. The biggest hurdle is letting go of control. It's okay if people come up with their own way of doing things as long as the work is getting done.

> *What would you do differently if you were to start a new blog/online business today (and couldn't leverage your existing audience)?*

First, I would limit the advice I take from all the gurus online and I would restrict my time in Facebook groups. While it's a good idea to network, I think most people get stuck in analysis paralysis and never actually start. In fact, that happened to me in the beginning, too. So here is your permission to stop!

Second, I would listen to my intuition a bit more. I think I've passed on some great opportunities in my business because I didn't think it was the right thing to do based on other people's opinions around me. Remember, it's your business, and you make the rules.

Third, I would join a paid mastermind sooner but be very selective and research it first. Ask other people who have been in the mastermind to get their feedback. Masterminds have been one of my biggest sources of business growth. It's amazing to have cheerleaders in your corner each week!

> *Looking back now, what is something you worried about/spent too much time doing that wasn't important down the road?*

So many things! If I had to choose just one, it would be trying to grow several platforms at once. A lot of us call this "shiny new object syndrome," and boy, do I have it bad. I still get caught up in it from time to time, but I've gotten better. I used to believe I had to be everywhere to grow my business. But all it did was burn me out and provide limited results.

What was the biggest obstacle you faced in building your business to where it is today? How did you overcome it?

Time is my biggest obstacle and I suspect that's true for many moms. We just added a second baby to the family so it's like starting again with juggling my family and business. But I've learned a lot and can give a few helpful tips on how to make things work.

First, communicate with your significant other about your needs and don't be shy. It's hard for other people to understand why you are spending so much time on something with little to no payoff in the beginning. You must be your biggest cheerleader and ask for what you need.

Second, schedule your work time on your calendar. Before I was making enough money to contribute to the family, I had to put my work time on our family calendar. This meant my husband knew I was not on mommy duty, I was working.

Third, when it's your time to work, leave the house if you can. For example, visit a library or coffee shop.

Fourth, if you can schedule a short "staycation" for yourself in a hotel room, it will do wonders when it comes to gaining traction in your business.

Time is always a struggle, but the more open I am about what I need, and the more intentional I am with my work time, the easier it has become.

What's your advice for bloggers who are still struggling?

Don't be afraid to do things your way. I think a lot of times I see bloggers get stuck in the cycle of chasing the newest trends and it ends up sending them in circles. Everyone's journey with blogging is different. There is no "one size fits all" strategy. If you tune out all the noise around you, you'll find you enjoy blogging more and it will become easier!

How can readers connect with you?

Readers can find out more at my website, RedefiningMom.com. You can also connect with me on Facebook, Twitter, Instagram, Pinterest, and YouTube.

CHAPTER 4: HOLLY REISEM HANNA

Learning to keep a positive mindset and push forward when times are tough will be imperative to your success.

Holly Reisem Hanna is the publisher and founder of the award-winning website, The Work at Home Woman, which helps women find remote careers and businesses that feed their souls. The content is not only motivational, but it provides straightforward, actionable steps that you can put into practice. If you are looking to work from home, this is the blog for you.

What is your favorite business book and why?

One that I always refer back to is *The 4-Hour Workweek* by Tim Ferriss. This book focuses on having a lifestyle business, which is the main reason I started a blog in the first place. I wanted to stay home with my daughter and earn an income, but I didn't want to trade hours for dollars. Tim's book talks a lot about mindset, time, automation, and living life to the fullest. The book is also filled with a ton of practical information and resources for new business owners.

How long did it take from starting your blog/online business until you were consistently earning $8,000 per month or more?

For a long time, I ran my blog and worked as a freelance social media manager. While I loved the steady income of the freelance gig, I think dividing my focus held me back from achieving financial success with my blog sooner. I didn't start earning $8,000-plus, per month, until my blog was six years old.

What single strategy or habit had the biggest impact on your business when going from zero to $100,000?

There were a few things that happened in my life. One, my daughter went to school full-time which gave me more time to focus on my blog. Two, I decided to invest in the blogging course, Elite Blog Academy, which gave me a detailed roadmap for taking my blog to the next level. Three, I started being more strategic in my marketing efforts and began to focus more on email marketing and building my list.

What new habit or routine has most improved your life in the last year?

I've always pushed myself hard, and in 2017, I ended up burning myself out.

So in 2018, I've been learning to manage my time better with block scheduling, and I've been making self-care a priority. It's amazing how much I can accomplish with block scheduling.

I use the Erin Condren Life Planner and schedule in all my daily activities from work and exercise to errands and social engagements. We all get the same 24-hours, but it's how we use it that matters, and with block scheduling, you can visually see if an activity will fit into your day or not.

I've also started doing yoga twice a week. It's one hour during which my brain completely shuts off, and I can entirely focus on my body and breathing. It not only keeps me fit, but it also keeps me sane.

When did you hire your first virtual assistant or other help? What advice would you give new bloggers regarding outsourcing?

I hired a virtual assistant a few months after I started my blog. I was going on vacation and wanted to unplug, so I hired a gal to watch over everything while I was away. From there, I started utilizing a VA on a regular basis. Today, I have a VA, a web programmer, and a team of writers.

When you start your search, be sure to vet the individual and contact their references. I've worked with my fair share of lousy freelancers, and I've found that the deeper you dig into their work history, the easier it is to weed out the bad ones from the good ones.

| *What would you do differently if you were to start a new blog/online business today (and couldn't leverage your existing audience)?*

I would start building and nurturing my email list immediately. When I started out, I knew I needed to send out a newsletter, but I didn't fully understand why it was so important. I was more excited by social media and focused my energy there. Well, algorithms changed, and what was once a good source of traffic slowly disappeared. With email marketing, you own your list, and you can engage and connect with your subscribers at any time.

| *Looking back now, what is something you worried about/spent too much time doing that wasn't important down the road?*

When I started my blog, I had a work-at-home forum. It was a beast to manage, and it didn't have a good ROI, in fact, it had a negative ROI. For years, I kept it going because I had so many forum members. After years of working on the forum, I finally decided to shut it down, because it wasn't producing the results I wanted.

The takeaway is, don't hold on to something that isn't working. Let it go and focus on something new or something that is producing the results you want.

| *What was the biggest obstacle you faced in building your business to where it is today? How did you overcome it?*

Getting used to extreme ups and downs. Technology and algorithms are continually changing, and you may be riding the wave one day, and the next the surfboard has been pulled out from under you.

Ebbs and flows are natural in business; it's how you react to them that matter. Learning to keep a positive mindset and push forward when times are tough will be imperative to your success.

It's also important to push yourself when times are good, because the ride will only last so long.

What's your advice for bloggers who are still struggling?

Find your tribe. There are going to be so many ups and downs in your blogging business. Being part of a like-minded group of people where you can ask questions, get recommendations, and vent is going to be so important on your journey.

How can readers connect with you?

Readers can find out more at my website, TheWorkatHomeWoman.com. You can also connect with me on Facebook, Pinterest, Twitter, Instagram, and LinkedIn.

CHAPTER 5: DAVE STUART, JR.

Those things haven't mattered much to my long-term success—writing helpful things has. That's it.

D ave Stuart, Jr. and his family live in a small town in Michigan where he teaches high school by day—his first vocational passion—and writes blog posts for teachers as time permits. He has been teaching for 11 years and blogging for six.

What is your favorite business book and why?

My favorite business book is *Essentialism* by Greg McKeown. McKeown gets to the heart of the power of focusing our efforts. I think my business success has been the result mostly of providence, but beyond that it has happened because I have chosen to be good at a few important things.

How long did it take from starting your blog/online business until you were consistently earning $8,000 per month or more?

It took four years for my online business to reach that point.

What single strategy or habit had the biggest impact on your business when going from zero to $100,000?

The biggest habit was deciding that I would publish a new blog post every Tuesday and Saturday, without fail. This forced me to produce a volume of work that led to the intellectual breakthroughs that made it possible for me to create the in-person workshops, keynote speeches, books, and products that my business is built on. These blog posts are also a massive array of freely available information, and this has allowed teachers around the USA and the world to find my work and determine if it can help them.

What new habit or routine has most improved your life in the last year?

In the last year, I would say the habit that has improved my life the most would be getting enough sleep each night. When I slip away from this habit, I find that the quality of my thinking decreases, and everything suffers as a result. The key to making this habit happen for me has been exercising the discipline of going to bed on time.

When did you hire your first virtual assistant or other help? What advice would you give new bloggers regarding outsourcing?

I hired a virtual assistant when I was about three years into the business, and this first VA was a wonderful, intelligent professional from the Philippines. I ultimately did not gain much from this experience because I was so bad at using the VA, keeping her queue filled, etc. This is still a struggle for me—how to better outsource the more repetitive tasks of my business (customer service, online course onboarding, etc.). I'm hoping to get better at this in the months to come.

What would you do differently if you were to start a new blog/online business today (and couldn't leverage your existing audience)?

Just like when I started out, I think I would select a pressing problem for teachers and write strictly and voluminously about that problem. Back when I started in 2012, that problem was implementing the Common Core standards. I think that the topics I write about today—which tend to be wide-ranging but loosely along the themes of inner work, student motivation, and literacy—would not be suitable for developing that initial audience.

Picking a problem and exhaustively writing about it develops something inside of you, as a writer, that makes later writing better and more powerful. It increases your ability to persist in the face of challenge. So I would select a problem—maybe teacher attrition, or curriculum creation, or debunking edu-fads—and write aggressively toward it. In my first months blogging in 2012, I had no publication schedule, but I would often produce one post per day. I would aim for a similar intensity. It would be all about getting the reps in.

One thing I would definitely do sooner would be making it easy for people to subscribe to my blog updates via email. I started doing that too late, about one year into blogging.

> *Looking back now, what is something you worried about/spent too much time doing that wasn't important down the road?*

Putting images with my blog posts and obsessing over Twitter followers. Those things haven't mattered much to my long-term success—writing helpful things has. That's it.

> *What was the biggest obstacle you faced in building your business to where it is today? How did you overcome it?*

The biggest obstacle became time. As someone who has no desire to quit his day job of high school teaching, but who also wants to expand his impact through online business, I began facing the bottleneck of my own time. For the first five years of my business (i.e., basically all of it), I earned most of my income through in-person speaking events at schools and conferences. The trouble with this is that I started counting up how many nights I was spending away from my family. It was 30 nights for two years in a row, an entire month of being away! Even though these nights away were giving us a greater income, they were costing me something I wasn't willing to pay—time away from my wife and kids during a precious phase of our lives.

So, I wrote a book—*These 6 Things: How to Focus Your Teaching on What Matters Most*—for a traditional publisher, and I built a helpful online course for teachers called The Student Motivation Course. Both of these took a lot of time to make, but they were geared at getting me off the road and back at home where I wanted to be. At the time of this writing, these appear to have been good bets, as these income streams look to eclipse speaking for the first time in the history of my business.

What's your advice for bloggers who are still struggling?

Write 100 helpful, reader-centric blog posts as quickly as you can. Fret not about web design. Just make sure you're treating your reader like you'd like to be treated. I don't use pop-ups. This certainly costs me blog subscribers. But I know that I don't meaningfully subscribe to blogs because I saw a pop-up. I subscribe because I want that person's brain in my inbox. I'm fully capable of figuring out how to subscribe to a blog, without the intrusion of a pop-up.

One of the earliest mantras I learned (I think it was from Pat Flynn) was to make the Internet better. This doesn't mean copying and pasting the latest conversion tactics from X blog onto yours. It means writing really useful, helpful things, and lots of them.

If writing 100 earnest blog posts fails, consider starting a new blog. You'll be starting from a much wiser, more experienced place than the one you were at 100 posts ago.

How can readers connect with you?

Readers can find out more at my website, DaveStuartJr.com. You can also connect with me on Twitter.

CHAPTER 6: TERRA DAWN

When I focused on the entire picture, and not each individual problem, I was able to create a solution that solved close to everything.

Terra Dawn is the blogger and owner of Uncork Your Dork and the Wham! Bam! Business Plan! membership site. In addition to sticking out like a sore thumb in her industry, she's hell-bent on teaching other online creatives how to launch their first few (yes, more than one) subscription products. When she's not creating amazing content, you can find her on her couch...watching every cartoon known to the eighties.

What is your favorite business book and why?

My all-time favorite business book (and trust me, I've read them all) is *Rhinoceros Success* by Scott Alexander. It's a book you can finish in one night, and you will immediately think is the cheesiest thing you've ever read in your life. But what you don't realize is that you've just read one of the most inspiring business books ever. Since reading it over a year ago, it's become easy to "be the rhinoceros." The little or large issues that pop up in my everyday business life simply become "something to barrel through." I *am* a rhinoceros.

How long did it take from starting your blog/online business until you were consistently earning $8,000 per month or more?

That is such a great question. It took me around three years. I started my business in 2015. But, I didn't start my business right. I began like most business owners with no direction, no focus, and no clear idea of how this whole thing was supposed to come together. Where I started in 2015 is the opposite of where I am now. If I'd had the guidance I have now, I probably could have created the same income in a much shorter time.

The problem with that, though, is that every person's business is a different journey. The courses, mentors, and lessons that I learned from are not the same ones that someone else who walks the exact same path will benefit from. Business owners come from different backgrounds, learning styles, and personalities. So their business journey is going to be unique every single time.

> *What single strategy or habit had the biggest impact on your business when going from zero to $100,000?*

Focusing on one domino in my business.

When I started out, I clung to everything I could when it came to success. Articles and emails talking about the thousands of dollars other bloggers were making in a month. Courses that I thought would change my life overnight. Ebooks that I thought would increase my list size by gang busters.

I. Tried. Everything.

It wasn't until March of 2017 that I realized I was focusing on what I wanted the outcome to be, but not what I needed to be doing to get there. I was taking every one of my personal pain points and I was trying to solve each one individually.

I wasn't making enough money, so I was creating courses and ebooks out the wazoo.

No time to focus on launches? I was doing the bare minimum before getting distracted and turning to another product.

I had goals, but absolutely no focus.

Then (due to a well-placed, last minute financial crisis) I was forced to focus on the bigger picture. Everyone's path is different, but for me my path led to creating one all-encompassing product with a recurring revenue system.

When I focused on the entire picture, and not each individual problem, I was able to create a solution that solved close to everything.

> *What new habit or routine has most improved your life in the last year?*

Planning my quarters. This was something I didn't understand for far too long. Online business revolves around content. Social media content. Product content. Blog content. Group content. It's insane the amount of content we must produce regularly!

When you sit back and plan your monthly content around themes and launches, you get a super clear idea of what is going well, plus you can reinforce lessons for your readers. Before I began planning my content, I found myself creating scattered messages. A post on Facebook wouldn't align with the message I was putting up on the blog or inside of Instagram. It was taking me longer to create the content simply because I was creating new content for every platform instead of repurposing.

Planning my quarters has given my readers a path to follow through my business and leads them to my solutions.

> *When did you hire your first virtual assistant or other help? What advice would you give new bloggers regarding outsourcing?*

I first hired my VA, Monica, at the end of 2017. I think I hired her at the perfect time, but I kinda wish I'd found her sooner...if that makes sense. Since hiring her, I've been able to add more help to keep my membership site running smoothly.

Do not hire someone unless you absolutely need them. I know that can be hard to figure out. I went through a few great team members because I thought I needed a team when I didn't.

When you first launch a business, you're going to be all things. You'll wear every hat in the biz. And this is a good thing. You need to figure out what you love and what you absolutely can't stand or simply don't have the time for. When you're at the point when you can truly say, "This is slipping to the wayside because there is simply too much for me to do," that's when you should start trying to work on your team.

As those "holes" have popped up in my own business, I've filled them with positions like IT, Social Media Manager, and Affiliate Manager.

> *What would you do differently if you were to start a new blog/online business today (and couldn't leverage your existing audience)?*

When I first started out, I focused on the small things. The PDF opt-ins. The blog's design. Products that weren't researched. It was a lot of wasted time. Instead, I should have focused on making connections with other bloggers to build my list and get my message out there. You can update your blog every day. But if you aren't working to make those connections, you won't get far very quickly.

| *Looking back now, what is something you worried about/spent too much time doing that wasn't important down the road?*

I wouldn't focus so hard on creating an audience of just anyone. For a while, I was super focused on creating downloads and blog posts to increase my list numbers. What I've learned is that it isn't about the list size. It's about how focused that list is. (There's that word again—focus.) Are you sending them consistent updates and information without holding back?

In the beginning, I was so focused on getting those numbers up that I overlooked the people those number represented. They weren't dedicated to my topic and worse yet, they weren't dedicated to me. I've since deleted close to 45 percent of my list, but it's more engaged and active than ever. I make 10 times the sales and get 10 times the excitement as a response to my weekly newsletters!

| *What was the biggest obstacle you faced in building your business to where it is today? How did you overcome it?*

Math! By far, math. I have a learning disability, dyscalculia, which makes finances, analytics, and time management more than a little bit difficult. Unfortunately, these are all super important when running a small business. (The IRS probably wouldn't take "I can't do math" as an excuse for not paying taxes.)

I wasn't diagnosed until college, so learning to live with this is fairly new to me. I've had to research new ways to stay ahead of my finances, and tools to keep everything organized. I've had to build daily habits around the areas I struggle with. I look at my finances for 10 minutes every morning and ensure my analytics are easily accessible in an Airtable spreadsheet. And I've had to find and fall in love with tools that fill the areas of my business that need major help.

I've also had to work with the emotional impact it's had on me. My confidence level was below zero 10 years ago. And although I wouldn't call myself a mathematician nowadays, I would say I'm much more comfortable asking questions and trying to understand the numbers in the moment.

| *What's your advice for bloggers who are still struggling?*

Business is not about being perfect! In fact, only entrepreneurs who can recognize their weakness and work to either overcome them—or hire a team to help them—will survive. If I were to ask you "What are you struggling with in business?" and your response was "Nothing, my business is great!" Then I guarantee you're about to fall flat on your face.

Business is all about the struggle. It's all about the fight. If you don't see any area where you can improve, then you're driving the small business bus with your eyes closed, my friend.

So, embrace your struggles and your imperfections. Those are what will make your business and help it grow.

How can readers connect with you?

I would love to connect! The quickest way to connect is via the Uncork Your Dork Facebook group. (Just give us a search. We are super easy to find.) If you want to take advantage of the free courses and opt-ins we offer, or join us inside the Wham! Bam! Business Plan! Academy, then head over to the blog at UncorkYourDork.com.

CHAPTER 7: CHRISTINA SCALERA

I started creating specific products that people wanted, and the demand has been incredible.

Christina Scalera is the attorney and founder behind The Contract Shop, a contract template store for creative entrepreneurs, wedding professionals, and coaches.

Four years ago, Christina found herself dreaming of pursuing a more creative path, and she started looking for alternatives to her in-house legal job. She explored everything from teaching yoga to becoming a freelance graphic designer to opening an Etsy shop.

In the process, she ended up coming full circle by creating a business that brought the benefit of her legal training to help her fellow creatives.

When she's not staring at a computer or awkwardly standing on café chairs for the perfect overhead latte photo, you can find her in the woods doing things that are sometimes dangerous but always fun, like riding horses, skiing, and reluctantly camping.

▍What is your favorite business book and why?

Tools of the Titans is my favorite business book. I didn't want it to end. I actually can't stand the bro-tastic podcast show Tim Ferriss puts on, even though I love him and his books. This book was the answer for someone like me who would prefer to cozy up to Tim sans the fluff and ads on air. I loved how he broke it down into different sections, like health, business, tech trends, and more.

The entire second part of the book, "Wealthy," was gold for business owners.

> *How long did it take from starting your blog/online business until you were consistently earning $8,000 per month or more?*

Consistently? We're just now getting there. Traditionally, for the past three years, I've run a semi-annual sale that has boosted our annual revenues and put us at or above that point each month. Until recently, I've been stuck in the feast/famine cycle and it wasn't until 2018 that this changed. We just had our first six-figure month, which was crazy. It doesn't feel real because I barely work on the stuff you see on my site. I'm working (or at least trying to) on the high-level stuff, the templates themselves or future developments.

> *What single strategy or habit had the biggest impact on your business when going from zero to $100,000?*

I can't say it's just one. There are so many things that have been combined to create this effect. If I had to pick one thing though (and this is kinda cheating, you'll see why in a minute), it's who I've associated with.

I've been really fortunate to connect with companies like HoneyBook, influencers like Jenna Kutcher and her mastermind and to develop a team that is just way better than I could ever be on my own.

These are companies and people I love from a consumer standpoint. I use HoneyBook in both my businesses. And I was a fan and user far before we ever collaborated, and even before they purchased the Rising Tide Society (who I also collaborated with before they merged with HoneyBook).

I only collaborate with companies and people I really want to serve. You know when someone does something for you and you are just so grateful? You think, "How am I ever going to repay this favor?" That's how HoneyBook, Rising Tide Society, Jenna and the gals in Jenna's mastermind make me feel. So, it's easy to go above and beyond and serve them. It's almost like a compulsion.

Now, this isn't to say you should just sit back and let these partnerships come to you. You need to get out there and find your happy place of people!

I never would have personally connected with Jenna by simply reading her blog and listening to her podcast. I met her at Bonnie Bakhtiari's Illume Retreat, which was a financial stretch for me at the time. But I took a leap of faith that something would come out of it. (Side note: About half the attendees ended up hiring me as their lawyer and becoming some of my first customers in The Contract Shop®. Thanks, Bonnie, I owe ya!)

I wasn't strategizing how I would meet people at Illume. In fact, I failed at that from the start. I couldn't even talk to Bonnie when I met her! I was fangirling hard. But I did strategically choose that retreat above others. It was more intimate and it was all inclusive, but most importantly, Illume had instructors I knew I wanted to be like and get to know. Connecting with the right people takes work, but it can really pay off in your business.

What new habit or routine has most improved your life in the last year?

This is going to sound dumb...but making the bed. Just looking in and seeing a bed made every time I pass the bedroom brings me so much joy. I guess that's a sign that I'm getting old. But seriously, I think it's part of a bigger habit, which is striving to do things in the moment.

When I first started my business, I was behind on everything. Laundry, dishes, cleaning but also business tasks like email, customer support, creating products, blogging, newsletters—you name it! I learned that to stop putting things off, you have to do them now. Even if that means it's not perfect or the "best version" of how you could do something. If you can answer an email in under two minutes, you should do it now, or ask them to set up a call (preferably with a link to your online scheduling tool like Calendly). I can't take credit for this example, though. I learned that specifically from Shanna Skidmore.

You can apply this to your whole life. Look at dishes. How long does it take to get them done? Ten minutes, tops? Yet, we'll (err, the "old" me would, at least) let them sit there for two days because we don't feel like doing it. Whereas, if you put each dish in the dishwasher when you're done with it, you don't have a pile to tackle later. Plus, you have a clean sink and clean dishes in the meantime. I don't know why I used to think cleaning was so lame. I hardly even notice I'm doing it anymore.

When did you hire your first virtual assistant or other help? What advice would you give new bloggers regarding outsourcing?

My first hire is still with me, albeit in a different role. Soon after I gave the first Rising Tide Society webinar, I was swamped. It got to be overwhelming, and I remember logging in to Heather Crabtree's Savvy group on Facebook during a "Share and Care Tuesday." Julie Painter had posted her VA services and I liked her branding. That was it. That's how I made my first hire. I love Julie, and she manages all our podcast guests on Creative Empire. However, I don't recommend a VA be your first hire.

It was for me, because everyone told me, "Oh, a VA is where you should start!" I wish I hadn't followed that advice because the first three months Julie was with me, she never met her hours. I had no idea what to give her or how to outsource. I felt bad giving her tasks even though it was her job and she was begging me for work. (I still feel bad asking contractors to do more work for me. There are some things you never get over!)

At the time, I had much more pressing needs than admin work. I think admin work comes much later for most of us. For example, it was taking me 12-plus hours per day to design PDFs, graphics, freebies, blog/Pinterest images and presentations, and then I'd have to do all my work on top of that for two companies. One of my first hires should have been a graphic designer to take that off my plate. But it's tough to find a graphic designer who does retainer work. If you're under-booked and underpaid, consider advertising yourself as such! You'll be flooded with people like me begging you for help.

My advice would be to hire out the tasks that are taking the most time, especially if you're just okay at them. I like designing. It makes me feel creative. I like to know what my customers are up to in Photoshop all day and understand the things they are struggling with. I like sharing those inside jokes with them. But, at the end of the day, there are only so many hours in a day. I was better suited to dabbling on the weekends and leaving The Contract Shop® design work to the pros.

> *What would you do differently if you were to start a new blog/online business today (and couldn't leverage your existing audience)?*

Oh, just roll over and give up, what's the point? No! Just kidding. Do *not* do that.

If I were starting over, the audience wouldn't matter, I'd find them. I'd find three people as "mentors" and follow their every move like a fangirl until they noticed me.

If they accepted me, I'd create a partnership with them and get in front of their audience, maybe via a newsletter swap or being a guest on their podcast. If they did not accept me, I'd find a new person and rinse/repeat until I found my three. Then I'd leverage the relationships from there. This isn't using people. I've followed this strategy and some of my connections are now my best friends. Plus, as my platform eclipses some of theirs, it's fun to support them in the way they did for me. This is business, but business can be personal, too.

Looking back now, what is something you worried about/spent too much time doing that wasn't important down the road?

Oh, goodness. Designing a website that wasn't optimized for conversions. I spent too much time making sure it was pretty, without paying attention to how and what people used it for.

What was the biggest obstacle you faced in building your business to where it is today? How did you overcome it?

Money. Isn't that the case for everyone? You feel like if you could just invest in this one thing, you'd finally make it. I overcame this by producing products people want. For a long time, I was stuck on making a course. Everyone said that's the way to make it online. So that's what I tried. But I kinda took a stab at what I thought people could use, without properly developing the content or the marketing, and was disappointed with the result. I figured I was bad at this online business thing. Then, I started creating specific products that people wanted, and the demand has been incredible. I'm so fortunate this is my career now. I'm glad I didn't give up.

What's your advice for bloggers who are still struggling?

Write about something people want. Stop trying to flatter yourself. No one cares about you until you give them a reason to. Once you've established a relationship with your readers, you can begin to build your full personality online by bringing in bits of you they haven't "met" yet.

How can readers connect with you?

Come say hi at TheContractShop.com. Use the big ol' search bar at the top to find something you need! Also, follow me on Instagram—it's where you will get an inside dive into my mind.

SECTION TWO

Habit Two: Create Systems for

Success

CHAPTER 8: CREATE SYSTEMS FOR SUCCESS

Successful people create systems so that essential tasks always get done.

Have you ever set a resolution to get fit or lose weight? Did you achieve your goal? If you answered yes to both questions, then you're unusual. Most of us fail to meet our goals even though we know exactly what we need to do—eat less and exercise more.

Habit one is important. Meaningful goals and strategy are the foundation of success. However, many people know what they need to do and still fail to meet their goals. This is because either they don't follow through or there's a flaw in their strategy.

Habit two addresses both these problems. It makes it easier to take consistent action. It also provides feedback on what's working and what's not working.

Systems help you take the required action no matter what happens. Systems aren't just about automation. They also include daily or weekly routines, outsourcing, accountability, measuring progress, investing in education, and more. We discuss the systems used by successful bloggers later in this chapter. But first I want to talk about willpower.

If you don't have systems, then you must rely on willpower to get things done. Let's return to our losing weight example. Say you decide to exercise five times a week but don't decide when, how, or where to do this. Each day you must decide when to exercise, what to do, where to do it, and who to exercise with.

Research shows that our willpower has limits. And while some lucky people may have more willpower than others, we all eventually make the easy choice and skip an exercise day.

In a research study published by the National Academy of Sciences, psychologists examined more than 1,100 parole hearing decisions made by U.S. judges. They found that the most influential factor in whether someone was granted parole wasn't their crime, background, or sentences. It was what time of day their case was heard.

> *"Prisoners who appeared early in the morning received parole about 70% of the time, while those who appeared late in the day were paroled less than 10% of the time."*

The study suggests that when judges make repeated rulings, they are more likely to rule in favor of the status quo. In short, we have limited willpower and repeated decisions erodes what willpower we have.

The answer is to create systems that reduce the amount of decision making and willpower needed to achieve our goals. In our losing weight example, systems might include:

1. Recruiting an accountability partner to exercise with.
2. Signing up for a competition or race, e.g. a half marathon or other event.
3. Hiring a personal trainer.
4. Signing up for an exercise class at a fixed time.
5. Creating a daily routine, such as exercising at a set place and time each day.
6. Tracking exercise time and weight loss or gain using a tracking app on your phone.

The first three systems all deal with accountability. They make sure you follow through. The fourth and fifth reduce decision making by determining in advance when and where you will exercise. The last system tracks your progress.

You need all three types of systems: accountability, execution, and tracking. We discuss specific systems for bloggers below. However, it's important to remember that we're all unique. What works for one blogger may not work for you. Be prepared to experiment. Try new things and figure out what helps you follow through and get results.

Also, don't abandon a system because it doesn't work out the first time. It may be enough to make minor adjustments. Meera Kothand, email marketing specialist and Amazon best-selling author of two books, shares this valuable advice:

> *Just because your offer doesn't sell like hotcakes the first time round or doesn't sell at all the first time round, doesn't mean that it's a lousy*

> *offer. It just means that you need to tweak and play around with the messaging of the offer until you get it right.*

ACCOUNTABILITY SYSTEMS

As a blogger, you enjoy the freedom to work when, where, and how you want. But this also means you have one big disadvantage over corporate employees. You don't have external accountability.

There's no boss telling you want to do. There are no shareholders or an executive board with expectations of you. You don't have a defined role, reporting structure, or performance reviews. And while this may sound appealing, it can also be a problem.

In a structured corporate environment, it's relatively easy to meet your goals. Even if you hate your job, you turn up each day, put in the time, and deliver what's required of you. But as a blogger, all sorts of temptations stand in your way. Whether that's spending an extra hour in bed, meeting a friend for coffee, or binge watching a Netflix show. There are endless reasons to avoid sitting down and getting the work done.

Accountability systems help you combat this effect. They keep you from giving up when the going gets tough. Below are some example accountability systems. Read them through, then pick one or more to try.

1. **Find an accountability partner**. Ideally this is someone with similar goals to you so that you understand each other's challenges. Meet regularly with your accountability partner to report progress and brainstorm solutions to problems.

2. **Join a mastermind group**. Masterminds are a group of people who meet virtually or in person to help each other reach their goals. You can join a paid or unpaid mastermind. The advantages of masterminds go way beyond accountability. In fact, their main function is so that members can receive input and support from their peers. The idea is that many minds are better than one.

3. **Share your goal.** If you're the kind of person who doesn't like letting others down, then share your goal (either with someone close to you or with a wider audience). Some bloggers publish their monthly income reports. This acts as a form of public accountability, motivating the blogger to share strong performance each month. If you don't want to share publicly, consider telling a close friend or spouse about your goals.

EXECUTION SYSTEMS

Okay, let's talk about execution systems. These can become your super power. Good execution systems compensate for your weaknesses and free you to operate in your zone of genius. They automate the important tasks so that they always get done, even when you encounter obstacles or feel like giving up.

Here're some execution systems used by successful bloggers.

1. **Create a content calendar** so that you know in advance what content you're going to publish and on what days.

2. **Outsource tasks to a virtual assistant or contractor**. Consider how you can outsource repetitive tasks, things you don't enjoy doing, or activities that take too long. Not only will these tasks always get done, you also gain time to spend on activities you love, or that have the greatest impact on the bottom line. Tasha Agruso, founder of the top-ranked DIY and home decor blog, Designer Trapped in a Lawyer's Body, said this about hiring help:

> *The best advice I have when it comes to hiring or outsourcing is this: Divide your monthly revenue by the number of hours you worked on your blog to determine your effective hourly rate. Then, for each task you perform, ask yourself if you would pay someone that amount of money to do the work. For example, if you determine that your effective hourly rate is $125 an hour, then ask, "Would I pay someone $125 an hour to schedule posts to Facebook?" If the answer is no, you need to outsource it to someone with a much lower hourly rate than your own.*

3. **Plan your time in advance**. There are many planning systems, so find the one that fits you and your schedule. You might plan out an entire week on Sunday night. Or you may prefer to plan each day the night before. Some bloggers design an "ideal week" which maps out what tasks get done on what days. This includes blogging tasks and personal activities, such as exercise, time with friends and family, etc. When you plan your time in advance, you're more likely to get the important stuff done and avoid wasting time.

4. **Batch related tasks**. This means blocking out an hour or more on your calendar to focus on one type of activity. For example, you might do all your writing on Tuesday and Thursday mornings. Or you may reserve one hour each day to answer emails. Batching helps maximize concentration and decrease distractions. Gina Horkey is a six-figure blogger and founder of Horkey HandBook, a website geared

toward helping others find or become a kickass virtual assistant. Here's how Gina plans her time:

> I try to pre-schedule my weeks on Sundays. I also keep a "model week," which outlines what I do on any given day Monday through Friday. The latter helps me to schedule meetings or appointments on the right days, enabling me to have more uninterrupted periods of work time.
>
> After my pre-scheduled appointments/meetings have been placed in my SELF Journal, I fill in the blocks of time that are left with my MITs— most important tasks. Ideally, I have no more than three MITs on any given weekday, making my to-do list manageable and keeping me focused.

5. **Adopt a morning ritual**. This strategy was popularized by Hal Elrod in his best-selling book *The Miracle Morning*. The purpose of a morning ritual is to make sure you take care of essential activities early in your day (when your willpower is highest). Your morning ritual might include any of the following activities: exercise, meditation or spiritual practice, reading, journaling, affirmations, visualization. We will talk more about some of these practices in chapter 14.

6. **Use automation tools**. Many bloggers automate common, repetitive tasks such as posting on social media, sending email sequences, and sharing sales messages.

7. **Create financial systems**. These ensure you manage your blogging income and expenses to achieve your goals. Several bloggers interviewed for this book recommend the *Profit First* system by Mike Michalowicz. Here's what Courtney Slazinik, six-figure blogger at Click it Up a Notch, says about *Profit First*:

> I now have a system in place to not only cover expenses and taxes but to pay myself twice a month and set aside money for just profit. At the end of each quarter, I can pull half or all the money out of the profit account as a bonus for our family. No longer do I have to check the bank account to make sure I have enough money to cover expenses before I pull out money. Now, that money goes into a separate account and I am able to pay myself.

Of course, there are many other execution systems. As always, I encourage you to explore these ideas and see what works for you. Identify critical tasks in your business and determine how best to systematize them. Be aware of your weaknesses and look for ways to compensate for them. For example, I struggle with repetitive tasks. So, I automate and outsource as many of these as possible. I also schedule my difficult work (such as researching and writing books) early in the day. This way I get my deep work done when I'm most alert and have maximum willpower.

Your formula will vary. Some people need more flexibility in their days and prefer not to over plan. That's okay. The key is to know yourself and leverage systems that help you follow through.

TRACKING AND IMPROVEMENT SYSTEMS

In habit one, we discussed acting with purpose. Doing more of what works and less of what doesn't. Tracking and improvement systems help you monitor your progress and observe the results of your actions. They show you what's having a positive impact in your business and what's not.

Focusing on your important tasks and ignoring distractions is central to your success. Kelly George, homeschooling mum and successful blogger at Fearless Homeschooling, says this:

> *I've ignored any number of shiny new things so that I can focus on the core of content, email subscribers, and customers. It's difficult not to jump on the latest bandwagon, but the effort has paid off. I may not have a huge Facebook following, but I do have happy customers who refer their friends.*

Tracking and improvement systems also keep you motivated. Some bloggers even share their progress publicly. This is another way to hold yourself accountable (see accountability systems above).

To start tracking your progress, first identify which metrics relate directly to your main goal. For example, if your goal is to earn $X per month from your blog, then you want to measure dollars earned each month. You can also track other metrics that drive earnings. Think about what measurable statistics relate to the main goal of your blog. Some options are:

- Page views (this can be found in Google Analytics).

- Unique visitors (also in Google Analytics).
- Email subscribers (this can be found in your Email Service Provider).
- Products or services sold in numbers or dollars.
- Operating expenses (know how much you're spending, not just how much you're earning).
- Net income.

I don't recommend obsessing over numbers. There are many vanity metrics you can ignore. Remember, if it doesn't directly relate to your goal then don't bother tracking it. Ask yourself, "Does this impact whether I'm achieving my main goal?"

Once you have a handful of metrics to measure, set up a weekly or monthly review process. For example, you could block out 30 minutes on the first Monday of each month. In that time, you update the numbers for the previous month and review changes. Take note of any significant movements up or down and make sure you understand what's causing the fluctuations. This is how you know what's working and what's not working in your business.

For example, if the number of visits to your blog jumps on a given day then (once you've finished celebrating) look at your Google Analytics for that day. Do you know which blog post or website pages were visited? Where did the visitors come from? Did the traffic also result in a higher number of conversions (e.g. new product sales or email subscribers)?

Knowing this information will tell you what kind of content your readers enjoy, which traffic sources are working for you, and what blog posts or strategies are driving conversions (and ultimately dollars earned).

Finally, act on the feedback. Tweak your strategy. Try new tactics. Do more of what's driving the results you want. And stop doing what isn't.

ACTION STEPS

1. Identify the essential strategic activities in your business. Focus on the ones that must happen every day, week, or year.

2. Decide which systems will help you stay consistent and follow through. Make sure you have systems in each of the following areas: accountability, execution, tracking, and improvement.

3. Implement the systems one at a time.

Remember, you can also combine systems. For example, I used to struggle with regularly publishing new articles on my blog. Here're some of the systems I've implemented to help me stay consistent:

– I have a content calendar. I plan my blog posts in advance, so I always know what needs to be published and on what days.

– The first thing I do each day is write for at least 30 minutes. This is a daily ritual. As an author and blogger, writing is my most important task. I prioritize it above everything else.

– I have a virtual assistant who manages my Pinterest account and schedules my blog posts. This way, I know new posts will be published and shared each week.

In the upcoming chapters, you will meet five bloggers who are succeeding online. Each person knows which activities create results in their business. As you read their stories, take note of the systems they have implemented and why. Also, visit their websites and see how they are putting these systems into action.

These bloggers have all learned what it takes to succeed and have generously shared their experiences. The following chapters are packed with insights, strategies, tactics, and advice that will help you create the business and life you dream about.

CHAPTER 9: GINA HORKEY

*I think showing up every day ready to dig in and do
the work is my "secret to success."*

G ina Horkey is a married, millennial mama to two precocious kiddos from Minnesota. Additionally, she's the founder of Horkey HandBook, a website geared toward helping others find or become a kickass virtual assistant. Gina's background includes making a living as a professional writer, an online business marketing consultant and a decade of experience in the financial services industry.

What is your favorite business book and why?

I don't know if I can pick just one, but my favorite recent read is *Work Less, Make More: The counter-intuitive approach to building a profitable business, and a life you actually love* by James Schramko.

Not only does James have a super inspiring story of how he went from being a collections phone agent to managing the largest luxury car dealership in Australia, but he packages all of his business knowledge into a guide to help other struggling business owners focus on the right things in order to scale. Working more isn't the answer, and building a profitable business around what you value in life is possible!

How long did it take from starting your blog/online business until you were consistently earning $8,000 per month or more?

I went from $0 to $4,000 in monthly revenue offering just services (freelance writing and virtual assistance) within six months of starting HorkeyHandBook.com.

I hit the $8,000 per month mark for the first time exactly 12 months after starting my business. It hasn't dipped below that since!

What single strategy or habit had the biggest impact on your business when going from zero to $100,000?

I think showing up every day ready to dig in and do the work is my "secret to success."

A lot of people say they want to build a successful business, but most of them don't want to actually do what it takes to get there. They may try for a while, but the first time life gets in the way, they stop and then have a hard time getting going again.

I knew that I wanted to change careers from the start and focused on the long-term goal of quitting my day job and running my own business full-time. I knew how much income I needed to make (roughly $5,000 per month) in order to just cover paying our bills (I was the only income generator) and broke the larger goal down into manageable chunks to stay motivated.

I've gone through many periods of wanting to give up or not feeling inspired. I've also gone through phases of burnout. When you're an executor, that's bound to happen. The difference for me is that I don't give in! I keep trucking despite the (business or personal) setbacks.

What new habit or routine has most improved your life in the last year?

Time blocking, hands down.

I try to pre-schedule my weeks on Sundays. I also keep a "model week," which outlines what I do on any given day Monday through Friday. The latter helps me to schedule meetings or appointments on the right days, enabling me to have more uninterrupted periods of work time.

After my pre-scheduled appointments and meetings have been placed in my SELF Journal, I fill in the blocks of time that are left with my MITs—most important tasks. Ideally I have no more than three MITs on any given weekday, making my to-do list manageable and keeping me focused.

Not every day ends up working out perfectly, but luckily I can try again the following day!

When did you hire your first virtual assistant or other help?

I made my first hire about 15 months after starting my business.

I wasn't looking to hire, but someone in my community (one of my students) brought a need to my attention and pitched herself as the solution. I agreed that it made sense, asked her rate and we moved forward.

While Mickey started as a Facebook group moderator, she now manages the blog for HorkeyHandBook.com. She maintains our editorial calendar, creates post images, works with guest posters and more!

I currently have half a dozen or so regular contractors working with me. I enjoy finding the right person for the job (i.e. a specialist), starting small and building the relationship from there.

What advice would you give new bloggers regarding outsourcing?

It's always easier to outsource before you're at max capacity.

Many people wait until they're too busy to hire help and then have a hard time delegating and training. Every business is different and each business owner wants things done to different specifications, so every virtual assistant needs some sort of training or orientation, even if they already know how to handle whatever service they're hired to do.

Besides hiring just before you're ready, I would say having the VA help to create SOPs (standard operating procedures) for any of the tasks they take on is smart. It doesn't have to be fancy. A Google Doc outlining the steps needed to accomplish the job will work. If you and the virtual assistant ever part ways or you promote them to another position, you'll be able to train someone new in in no time!

What would you do differently if you were to start a new blog/online business today (and couldn't leverage your existing audience)?

We're actually kind of doing it with KidsVsBikini.com.

While there might end up being some crossover, it's a completely different niche and we're not banking on our current site to do the heavy lifting. We will be leveraging our personal social media channels and existing family/friend relationships to get the initial word out, otherwise it'll be mainly smart social media (Pinterest/Facebook) strategy and SEO (search engine optimization).

This is taking into consideration that we'll be publishing relevant, valuable content. Beyond that, we'll be following a similar strategy of publishing consistently, building an email list and making products that our audience wants, which can help them accomplish their goals (being fit and healthy).

> *Looking back now, what is something you worried about/spent too much time doing that wasn't important down the road?*

Sometimes I think businesspeople (including myself) want everything to be perfect before they unveil it.

You want your website to be perfect before you launch it, for example, but launching it really just means hitting "publish." You want your sales page/funnel to be perfect before you make your product available to your audience, so you wait much longer than you should.

But it will never be perfect and even if it's close, it doesn't last long. Technology breaks, and information changes at the speed of light. You simply cannot stay stagnant.

I also remember hearing that your audience will let you know when something's wrong or it doesn't work properly. That's totally true! While you don't want to release a subpar experience or product, if something doesn't quite work, don't worry, you'll hear about it!

> *What was the biggest obstacle you faced in building your business to where it is today? How did you overcome it?*

I think it's wanting to give up when stuff feels hard.

I go through at least one period each year (it's probably a lot more!) during which I want to throw in the towel. Put my hands in air and say, "Peace out."

But I don't.

Instead, I take some time away to recharge and then I come back to it. Just imagine if I quit before my freelance business got off the ground. Or when I was creating my first online course. It'd be sad, because I would have missed out on a ton!

I wouldn't have been able to quit my day job. We wouldn't be able to travel south each winter as a family. I don't know what I'd be doing, but I can't imagine I'd have as much flexibility as I do now.

I also wouldn't be in the position to help so many others create their own lifestyle businesses. Starting a blog or offering services online is just the tip of the iceberg. There's so much opportunity that exists in online business, it's crazy!

What's your advice for bloggers who are still struggling?

Keep at it. Don't quit.

Think about where you want to go and figure out what it will take to get there. Break down your big goals into much smaller chunks and focus on hitting each one, one at a time.

Too often we measure our success against people who have much more time and experience on their side. People are successful at things (like blogging), because they first start. But then they hone their craft by "putting in their reps" and practicing. They continue to iterate over time, knowing that change is constant.

And lastly, they study (not copy) people ahead of them. They join masterminds. Hire a coach. Do what it takes to reach people on the next level and learn from them, often shortcutting their own process.

How can readers connect with you?

If offering services (freelancing writing, customer service, social media management, etc.) is your thing, feel free to check out my blog, HorkeyHandbook.com. I also offer a couple of online courses on the topic.

If Facebook is your thing, like my page. Regardless, I wish you the best of luck in your blogging journey. Why not YOU, and why not NOW?

CHAPTER 10: MEERA KOTHAND

The brands that will have the most success are those who are there continuously nurturing their audience and who don't neglect people just because they said no to buying something this time around.

Meera Kothand is an email marketing specialist and Amazon best-selling author of the books *The One Hour Content Plan* and *Your First 100*. Her goal is to make powerful marketing strategies simple and relatable so that solopreneurs and small business owners can build a tribe that's addicted to their zone of genius.

What is your favorite business book and why?

My favorite book was *Linchpin: Are You Indispensable?* by Seth Godin. I read it when I started entertaining thoughts about building my own business. Reading that book was the wakeup call I needed.

How long did it take from starting your blog/online business until you were consistently earning $8,000 per month or more?

It took me about two years to start making this amount consistently.

> *What single strategy or habit had the biggest impact on your business when going from zero to $100,000?*

Getting comfortable in my skin when it comes to selling and having the intent to want to make money. Selling doesn't have to be sleazy or uncomfortable or put your ideal buyer on the spot. When done right, selling can be almost effortless.

This boils down to a keen understanding of how your offer relates to your ideal buyer as well as the objections, false beliefs, and assumptions they have about themselves and in their abilities to solve this problem that your business or offer helps them with.

Selling is about helping your ideal buyer overcome all of that. It's almost woo, but I do feel that people can sense your hesitations when it comes to selling via email or through sales calls. The moment that hesitation is gone, your words come across bolder and you're more convincing. You're in business to help people with your skills, but you also earn a living from your business. So it's not wrong to have the intent to want to make money. These two shifts changed everything for me.

> *What new habit or routine has most improved your life in the last year?*

Sprints and batching have changed the way I work drastically. A sprint means that you're focusing on one project for a short intensive period of time. Batching is when you do more of a same task to save resources and time. I've always known the importance of these, but I've taken them up a notch in the last year. I've been able to complete projects a lot faster this way. And while the period of working on them is intensive, I'm able to enjoy longer breaks in between launches and projects.

> *When did you hire your first virtual assistant or other help? What advice would you give new bloggers regarding outsourcing?*

I started hiring help about six months into my business. While I don't have anyone full-time, I hire part-time help from designers and VAs pretty often.

My advice is to know what your strengths are. Know what you don't enjoy and which task doesn't lie in your zone of genius. Also look out for repetitive tasks in your business. The better an understanding you have of these, the easier it will be to start outsourcing. People say hiring full-time staff is a necessary move in order to grow. Honestly, it doesn't have to be that way if that's not the vision you have for your business.

What would you do differently if you were to start a new blog/online business today (and couldn't leverage your existing audience)?

I would create offers more quickly and get them out to my audience. I felt that I needed to provide value for a good six months before I offered my audience anything to buy. It felt like a rite of passage, as if I had to pay my dues. It doesn't have to be that way at all. Many people in your audience are further along in their journey toward understanding how your business can help them solve their problems. People who are further along in the customer journey will not hesitate to buy from you even if they've known your brand for only a short period of time. What matters is whether or not you're fulfilling a need. There's no right or fixed answer on how long you need to provide value before offering a paid product.

Looking back now, what is something you worried about/spent too much time doing that wasn't important down the road?

I worried too much about my products if they didn't sell as well as I wanted them to, especially in the beginning. I spent excessive amounts of time obsessing over the price and funnels when I should have been focused on thinking about how my audience was viewing the messaging I had built around my product. Just because your offer doesn't sell like hotcakes the first time around, or doesn't sell at all in the beginning, doesn't mean that it's a lousy offer.

It just means that you need to tweak and play around with the messaging of the offer until you get it right.

What was the biggest obstacle you faced in building your business to where it is today? How did you overcome it?

My biggest obstacle was mindset. Some people say they always knew they wanted to be entrepreneurs. Well, that wasn't me. No one in my family is an entrepreneur. Going to college, getting a degree, and getting a job was the norm. So I had to overcome a lot of self-doubt while building my audience. I often had questions such as "who am I?" and "why me?" I questioned my worth in what I had to share with my audience. Honestly, it's a work in progress. You can't fully overcome mindset issues, especially when they are woven into the fabric of who you are and the values you've been imbibed with since a young age. But you can definitely work on them and say NO when those thoughts start creeping back in.

What's your advice for bloggers who are still struggling?

Stay in it for the long haul. Marketing has changed. Customers are more wary. Your audience decides where they get information from and how they want to engage with your brand. The brands who will have the most success are those who are there continuously nurturing their audience and who don't neglect people just because they said no to buying something this time around.

How can readers connect with you?

Readers can find me on my slice of the Internet at meerakothand.com. If you're struggling with email marketing, I have a free email course available at meera.email/course.

CHAPTER 11: KELLY GEORGE

It's okay if it takes a while to get it right. While some are lucky enough to hit the right combination from the beginning, most people need to experiment and learn before they become successful.

Kelly George is a homeschooling mum of five children aged nine to 14. She's also a part-time entrepreneur in the homeschooling niche and a part-time nursing student. She travels with her family full-time, with no home base, which is why she started working online.

What is your favorite business book and why?

Deep Work by Cal Newport. I believe the claim that intense focus is the modern day superpower and an essential requirement for success. No one can produce quality work if they're checking Facebook every five minutes. Every time I read this, I find new ways to improve my work practices and get better results.

How long did it take from starting your blog/online business until you were consistently earning $8,000 per month or more?

I'm still not there consistently, but it took two years of up to 20 hours a week of work to consistently make a decent, reliable monthly income, although it could have been much faster. I aim to reach $8,000 per month by the end of 2018 while still working less than 20 hours a week. I'm using what I've learned with Fearless Homeschool to diversify and increase my passive income and start new niche sites until I reach the point where the seven of us can travel the world full-time.

What single strategy or habit had the biggest impact on your business when going from zero to $100,000?

Doing the most important thing. My hours are limited, so I have to make the most of them. I learned early on to set my most important task based on goals, then buckle down and actually do it. It's hard to build that discipline because the task is usually difficult and sometimes it's boring, so it's easy to get distracted or caught up in busywork.

Scheduling a pile of updates to Facebook is easy, but will have a negligible effect on my income. Spending an hour working on a sales page, a new product, or an event is difficult but will increase my income, so I have to do this instead. I've ignored any number of shiny new things so that I can focus on the core of content, email subscribers, and customers. It's difficult not to jump on the latest bandwagon, but the effort has paid off. I may not have a huge Facebook following, but I do have happy customers who refer their friends.

What new habit or routine has most improved your life in the last year?

Batching my work. It's consistent with the way of working that *Deep Work* promotes. Instead of spending small amounts of time on many different tasks, batching involves spending large chunks of time on one task. In practice, this means that I might spend all my work hours for a week writing an email sequence. I still check emails and do other important daily tasks, but only when my concentration is spent for the day.

Sometimes I'll block off a week where I won't check emails or social media at all. As a result, my output has increased exponentially without working extra hours. This is the only reason I finally managed to get my signature course, Zero to Homeschool, finished. It was taking forever so I didn't do anything else except that for weeks! Batching has reduced my stress, because I can see real progress on important tasks after every session. The visible progress also helps me switch off, so work doesn't take over my life.

When did you hire your first virtual assistant or other help? What advice would you give new bloggers regarding outsourcing?

I don't have a regular VA. Sometimes I feel like I should because everyone raves about them, but I dislike managing people to the point where I'd rather do it myself. I've been intentional in how I set things up, so everything I can automate is automated, and the rest, such as image creation and blog post uploading, is systematized so that it's as quick as possible. Checklists are essential for all standard tasks.

However, I do have some help. I outsource small tasks to freelancers. My husband is not techy at all but helps out with repetitive work, and I'm gradually training my eldest daughter in all areas of online business, so she's beginning to take some of the workload. I have affiliates to help me sell, and I also have a few freelance content writers working on a new project.

If you're going to outsource anything, you need to be incredibly clear about what you want or you're wasting everyone's time. Provide guidelines, a brand board, examples, and a clear description, otherwise you'll get something totally different than what you wanted, and it will be your fault.

What would you do differently if you were to start a new blog/online business today (and couldn't leverage your existing audience)?

I'm doing this now, and it's a lot of fun!

First, I'm making SEO a priority. I didn't spend much time on SEO with Fearless Homeschool because it seemed complicated and I already had so much to learn. I regretted it afterward because I missed out on a lot of traffic. My SEO traffic tripled in the first month I began paying attention to it, and it's increased steadily ever since. Thousands of missed visitors a month equals a lot of missed income.

Second, I'm making affiliate marketing a part of my blog from the beginning. I was focused on my courses with Fearless Homeschool and didn't consider affiliate marketing for the first year, but now that I do it, I'm a huge fan. As long as I can drive traffic to existing evergreen posts, which is easy and automated with Pinterest and SEO, it's a great way to start creating passive income from day one. Plus, I love not needing to worry about the sales and customer service side, let alone creating and hosting the product. Affiliate payments are like magic money appearing in my bank account, which is a lovely feeling.

> *Looking back now, what is something you worried about/spent too much time doing that wasn't important down the road?*

Social media. It's often portrayed as the magic ingredient that will get visitors and customers to your site, if you can just crack the code. I've found the time required is high, the click-throughs are low, and the requirements for success are mystifying and often change abruptly.

I stopped posting to Instagram in 2017 because even with 2,300-plus followers, my site traffic didn't justify the effort. I've shut down my Facebook group of nearly 1,000 members because it took so much time, but when I mentioned a post or product of mine, or an affiliate sale, it was essentially ignored. People were there for the tips and community so any "advertising" didn't register.

I now have a Facebook page and a Pinterest account that are mostly automated. They're both effective enough to justify their existence and are the only accounts I've started for my new online projects.

> *What was the biggest obstacle you faced in building your business to where it is today? How did you overcome it?*

Knowing what to do and how to do it. It's all so overwhelming. There are so many ways to blog, so many plugins and other programs. Which theme should I use? Which email software? Which course hosting? Should I write ebooks, produce courses, start a membership site, or focus on affiliate marketing? What should my niche be? And once you make any decision, there's a steep learning curve to follow. The choice is a blessing, but also a curse. I've just moved my courses to self-hosted, and while it's now a much better system it was a nightmare to choose the plugins, make sure they played nicely together, and learn how to use them.

To minimize overwhelm, I now have a system for narrowing down choices. Finally, once I've chosen, I move on. If I see an article now about self-hosting courses or a new course plugin, I don't even look at it. The decision has been made and it's final!

If you tend to agonize over your decisions, choose something that meets your needs now and commit to it for at least six months. Take note of other things that may suit, but don't intensively look at them until you're ready. Don't obsess over the details, just get the important things done first. Then you can worry about the polish. It's all related to doing the most important thing first. Generally the things I get bogged down in are not that important in the long run.

What's your advice for bloggers who are still struggling?

Step back and look at what you're doing, at all of your stats and feedback, and get honest about what's really working. If you only get 10 page views a month and no income from Instagram, abandon it. If your posts about vegetable gardening are really popular, but no one's interested in farmhouse style, learn from that. Don't feel like you have to do what everyone else is doing, just do what's actually working.

Also, don't be afraid to change direction. I had my first homeschooling blog for eight months before I worked out my current approach, and I shut that site and started Fearless Homeschool. Because it was based on experience, Fearless Homeschool grew very quickly. It's okay if it takes a while to get it right. While some are lucky enough to hit the right combination from the beginning, most people need to experiment and learn before they become successful.

How can readers connect with you?

In lots of ways! I'm always happy to chat. It depends what you're interested in.
I write about homeschooling at fearlesshomeschool.com.
I write about books for children at brilliantbooksforkids.com.
And everything else is at kellygeorge.net.

CHAPTER 12: COURTNEY SLAZINIK

Take it one day at a time. One task at a time. Pick a project, write down every actionable step that needs to be done for that project, and start plugging away.

As a former elementary school teacher, Courtney Slazinik has been able to combine her passion for photography and love of teaching to create her online business, Click it Up a Notch®. At Click it Up a Notch® Courtney helps people better understand their DSLR cameras through tutorials, ebooks, and online courses.

What is your favorite business book and why?

Profit First by Mike Michalowicz. For years I ran my business without completely understanding my finances. I always had enough in the bank to cover my expenses and taxes but I didn't truly pay myself. Instead, I would pull money out when we needed it, whether it was for a big family vacation or a large purchase. However, after reading *Profit First*, I now have a system in place to not only cover expenses and taxes but to pay myself twice a month and set aside money for just profit.

At the end of each quarter, I can pull half or all the money out of the profit account as a bonus for our family. No longer do I have to check the bank account to make sure I have enough money to cover expenses before I pull out money. Now, that money goes into a separate account and I am able to pay myself. I wish I had read this book when I first started.

How long did it take from starting your blog/online business until you were consistently earning $8,000 per month or more?

It took me about eight years to consistently make over $8,000 a month in gross revenue. Prior to that, I had months where I would make a five-figure income in that month because I had a large launch, but then the months during which I didn't launch a product were much slower. I had a few evergreen email sequences, but the income wasn't consistent. This can be challenging when you have large influxes of income. You need to make sure you are budgeting correctly to cover all your expenses on the months where the income is slower. Again, another reason I love *Profit First*.

What single strategy or habit had the biggest impact on your business when going from zero to $100,000?

Personally, I feel like I had two very different strategies. It took about five years to make over 100,000 in gross revenue. The first year I was able to do that was due to three successful launches. I had an online course that I only offered a couple of times a year. It was an open and close cart and the launches were vital to my business.

However, the type of workshop I was running required too much of my time. The workshop was a six-week course during which I provided individual feedback each week to photographers and it became too much. Not only was the course a lot of work, the launch leading up to the course was extremely stressful. I knew I needed to reach certain goals for each launch, so I would make enough money to cover expenses in the slow months. I realized this wasn't a lasting business model for me and my family.

During my seventh year, I set up an evergreen funnel that included a webinar. Evergreen refers to content that remains fresh over a long period of time. Having an evergreen funnel allows you to automate your sales process. You can sell your product 24/7 without needing to be present. Then I started doing joint webinars. I would team up with another person to teach and pitch to their audience. By having the evergreen webinar running in the background and hosting weekly live webinars to either my audience or someone else's, I was able to make a drastic change in my income.

Not only did my income increase, but I was able to do something that worked well and repeat it. No longer was I stressing about how to create new ways to launch or hoping I would hit my goal. I created a system that worked and then repeated it over and over again. The evergreen webinars and live webinars have become the backbone of my business. My community loves the webinars because even if they don't purchase what I share about at the end, they still get over 30 minutes of solid photography advice. I love being able to provide that extra value to my community.

What new habit or routine has most improved your life in the last year?

At the beginning of each week I try to do a "brain dump." I write down everything and every action step that is floating around in my brain that I want to or need to complete for the business. Then I go through the brain dump and decide what I want to or need to take care of for the week. Next, I'll pick three things for each day. This helps me get all the ideas on paper. By only picking three action items a day, I'm allowing myself to succeed and giving myself a manageable task because I know life will get crazy with three kids, and I cannot take on too much at once.

When did you hire your first virtual assistant or other help? What advice would you give new bloggers regarding outsourcing?

In the summer of 2016, we were moving yet again. I had already moved my business from Japan back to the states seven weeks after having my third child. I knew how much work I needed to put in to help my family adjust, unpack a house, and get settled. My number one priority has always been my family before the business. Since we had another move, I knew I needed help. I decided to hire one of my contributors to run the blog side of my business. She coordinated guest posts and formatted all the blog posts. I couldn't have gotten through that move with such an easy transition for my business without her. Earlier this year, I hired her as a full time VA to help with other projects in addition to the blog.

This past year, we also hired our first customer service representative. When I hired my VA, I approached her and asked if she wanted the job and lucked out that she was so amazing. I worried lightning wouldn't strike twice, so for this position I decided to put out an application and let people from my community apply.

The best advice I can give for hiring someone is treat it like a "real" job. I'm not saying what we do isn't a real job, but if you don't put people through a multi-step hiring process, you may hire the wrong person. One of my biggest fears when hiring people is having to fire them if they aren't a good fit. Thankfully, that hasn't happened.

We had a three-round process for the customer service position. First round was the application. We asked candidates questions about themselves and gave them a task to complete. We asked people to create a video for us by following step-by-step instructions that we provided. This showed us whether people could follow written directions which is how we often communicate. After we narrowed down the applications, we asked them to answer eight real emails we had received over the past year. Then, we invited a few people to do video interviews with us. It was a lot of work and took time, but we found the perfect person for the job. Plus, we kept several applications on file of other amazing candidates to choose from when another job pops up.

> *What would you do differently if you were to start a new blog/online business today (and couldn't leverage your existing audience)?*

If I had to start over and couldn't leverage my community, the first thing I would do is hire a business coach. I waited almost eight years before hiring one myself. I took course after course but it wasn't until I hired a coach that I saw the massive, consistent growth in my business that I wanted. I gained an additional benefit by learning from those who have gone before me and already made their own mistakes: I was able to use their shortcuts, too. It is quite an investment, but it is worth every penny. Set aside some of your profit and invest it back into your business and yourself with a business coach.

> *Looking back now, what is something you worried about/spent too much time doing that wasn't important down the road?*

Early on, I spent far too much time building my Facebook page only to have Facebook constantly change the algorithm. I wish I had taken that time and energy and put it into building my email list instead. That has been my number one focus for the past five years and it has paid off. Building that email community allows you to contact people when you want, instead of trying to learn a new algorithm each week.

> *What was the biggest obstacle you faced in building your business to where it is today? How did you overcome it?*

Time used to be a big struggle. When I started Click it Up a Notch® I had a three-year-old and a one-year-old. I was only able to work during nap time and in the evenings. This past year was the first year all three of my kids were in school and I could work uninterrupted all day. I realized in those early years that I couldn't keep working at night. I needed to spend time with my family and not constantly be at the computer. I started to put stricter boundaries on my time and taught my kids that sometimes I would be working while they were home. Now, after years of this, they know that I work and need time and space to complete my tasks.

What's your advice for bloggers who are still struggling?

Make a list of what you need to do. Pick three things to do today and tackle them. When you are struggling, the to-do list seems endless and you start to feel like you aren't making any traction. Take it one day at a time. One task at a time. Pick a project, write down every actionable step that needs to be done for that project and start plugging away. It is completely normal to struggle and want to quit. I want to quit about once a year. Remind yourself why you do what you do, make your list and start tackling it.

How can readers connect with you?

You can find me at ClickItUpANotch.com.

CHAPTER 13: TASHA AGRUSO

Few bloggers achieve the level of success they desire because they aren't willing to invest money to get the education they need. Those who invest the money and do the work (all the work—buying courses and ebooks you don't complete doesn't count) are the most successful.

Tasha Agruso is the owner and founder of the top-ranked DIY and home decor blog, Designer Trapped in a Lawyer's Body. She is also the creator of Designer in a Binder and the popular online course, Affiliate Marketing for Bloggers: The Master Course. She has happily retired from the private practice of law to blog full-time and lives in North Carolina with Joe, her firefighter husband, and their young twin daughters.

What is your favorite business book and why?

My favorite business book is *You Are a Badass* by Jen Sincero because it helped me overcome a lot of limiting beliefs that were holding me back in my business. Limiting beliefs are an entrepreneur's worst enemy. The sooner you identify your limiting beliefs and get over them, the better off you will be.

How long did it take from starting your blog/online business until you were consistently earning $8,000 per month or more?

It took me just over two years to build my blog to the point that I was consistently earning at least $8,000 per month.

What new habit or routine has most improved your life in the last year?

Over the past year, I have started focusing only on growing my earnings per unique visitor to my blog. This has helped me focus on the things that grow my revenue and ignore the vanity metrics that don't matter. I wish I had figured this out sooner. Far too many bloggers chase page views. But, at the end of the day, if you focus on growing your earnings with the blog traffic you already have, you will be better off.

I also set monthly and quarterly goals. Setting specific and measurable goals keeps me focused on tasks that will help me reach those goals. This makes it easier to ignore all the distractions.

When did you hire your first virtual assistant or other help? What advice would you give new bloggers regarding outsourcing?

I hired my first part-time assistant after I had been blogging over two years. It was the most difficult decision I had to make because one of the appealing things about blogging is the low overhead. I was stressed by the thought of taking on the expense of an assistant. But once I realized how much of my time it freed up to focus on the big picture (like growing my earnings per unique visitor), I wished I had done it much sooner. I spent too much time doing repetitive tasks that could have been done by someone else.

The best advice I have when it comes to hiring or outsourcing is this: Divide your monthly revenue by the number of hours you worked on your blog to determine your effective hourly rate. Then, for each task you perform, ask yourself if you would pay someone that amount of money to do the work. For example, if you determine that your effective hourly rate is $125 an hour, ask yourself, "Would I pay someone $125 an hour to schedule posts to Facebook?" If the answer is no, you need to outsource it to someone with a much lower hourly rate than your own.

What would you do differently if you were to start a new blog/online business today (and couldn't leverage your existing audience)?

I would start growing my email list immediately. I would also develop a product for my main audience much sooner. In my opinion, having an engaged email list and a product to sell will give you far more control over your business destiny than anything else.

Looking back now, what is something you worried about/spent too much time doing that wasn't important down the road?

Overall, I feel like the time I devoted to social media would have been much better spent on growing my email list. I was far too motivated to grow my social media numbers just because I felt like that's what I "should" be doing. But spending so much time on platforms that frequently change and could disappear completely is not the best use of any blogger's time.

What was the biggest obstacle you faced in building your business to where it is today? How did you overcome it?

My biggest obstacle was limited time. When I started my blog, I was still a full-time trial attorney and had a demanding schedule. Also, my twin girls were young at the time. To say I was busy is an understatement. It took grit and determination to stay up late and get up early every morning to work on my blog. But I was determined to succeed so that I could leave the private practice of law. That determination made me find the time and energy to make it happen. But time was a huge obstacle. Looking back, I don't know how I survived.

What's your advice for bloggers who are still struggling?

I believe that constantly educating yourself is vital to succeeding as a blogger.

A lot of bloggers want to earn money, but many aren't willing to invest in educating themselves to make that happen.

I spent nearly $80,000 to go to college and law school, and that was a bargain. I took out fewer student loans than almost everyone I know. Many of my friends racked up $200,000-plus in student loans. And you know what? I didn't know for sure that I would get a job when I graduated. And even if I did, I had no idea what my salary would be, or how long I would have the job. It was a risk. A really, really, really, expensive risk.

Cosmetologists, ultrasound technicians, automotive technicians, doctors, dental hygienists. They all invest in education before earning from their chosen field. And most invest thousands or even hundreds of thousands dollars to do it. That's how the world works. So why should blogging be any different?

The reality is that the blogging world isn't any different. Yet, few bloggers achieve the level of success they desire because they aren't willing to invest money to get the education they need. Those who invest in education and do the work (all the work—buying courses and ebooks you don't complete doesn't count) are the most successful.

For the first year or so that I was earning an income from my blog, I reinvested most of my earnings back into my business. I spent a large part of that money on education. I believe that investment has been a significant factor in my success. I continue to invest in my education every year.

How can readers connect with you?

You can read all about my home decor and DIY adventures at designertrapped.com.

SECTION 3

Habit 3: Believe in Yourself

CHAPTER 14: BELIEVE IN YOURSELF

Successful people accept responsibility for their results and believe in their power to achieve the desired outcome, no matter what happens.

With a solid strategy (habit one) and systems for success (habit two) you can achieve a lot. But sooner or later, you will hit a roadblock. This may be internal (fear, self-doubt, etc.) or external (such as a health issue or financial problem).

> To reach your **full potential** you must move past these obstacles. When the going gets tough, the successful keep going.

Habit three gives you the tools to push through the difficult times. It's all about adopting the right mindset.

Everyone has a set of ingrained beliefs. We tell ourselves stories about the situation we're in. Some of our beliefs hold us back. It may be our ideas about money—how much we deserve, our ability to earn, our spending or saving habits. Or it may be our beliefs about what we're capable of or what others think about us.

Luckily, your beliefs can be changed. If a thought is preventing you from achieving your goals, then replace it with a new belief. Create a different reality by changing the story you tell yourself. Nina Garcia is a successful blogger who founded Sleeping Should Be Easy, a go-to parenting blog and resource for moms of young kids. When I asked Nina which habit had the biggest impact when going from zero to $100,000, she said this:

> *Only when I changed my mindset from the blog as a side hustle to earning a full-time income did this change actually happen.*

Nina also went on to say:

> *Even now, each time I shift my mindset, I not only stretch myself beyond my comfort zone and grow as a person, I also grow the business.*

Habit three is something you will work on forever. Fortunately, there are many tools to help you do this. Let's look at some of the most popular ones.

GIVE UP THE BLAME GAME

Okay, this is less a tool and more a state of mind. To be successful, you must accept responsibility for your results. If you already believe that you get what you deserve, then skip ahead to the next section. But if you've ever thought any of the following, then please keep reading:

> *1. If only my spouse didn't do [thing], then I'd be able to go after my dreams.*
> *2. The economy is so bad right now, I'm never going to find the job I want.*
> *3. It's not fair. I had a [bad/poor/difficult] upbringing, it's so much harder for me to get [thing].*
> *4. I can't do [thing] because of my [health/age/gender].*
> *5. I can't do what I want because I must take care of my [kids/elderly parent].*

In each of these examples, the obstacle is an external factor—whether it's your spouse, upbringing, health, or a dependent. I understand that some of us are dealt a tougher deck of cards than others. And while this is unfair, lamenting the problem is not the solution.

There are many examples of successful bloggers who have overcome difficult circumstances, such as Jon Morrow of SmartBlogger.com. Jon has a neuromuscular disorder called Spinal Muscular Atrophy. He lives in a wheelchair and can only move his face. Yet, despite incredible challenges in his life, Jon has built a blogging empire and reached over five million people.

Jon didn't blame his situation. Instead, he turned it to his advantage. He used his determination to overcome challenges and to propel himself far beyond the average person.

This is what you need to do, too. Start practicing today. Every time you find yourself blaming something external, stop and ask yourself this important question:

> What else can I do in this situation?

For example, say you're stuck in traffic and are late for an important meeting. Your first reaction is to feel frustrated and blame the traffic. But instead, think about how you can see the situation differently. Can you turn on some relaxing music or listen to a podcast? Can you use this time to remember the things you are grateful for? You have a job, a car, a meeting to go to. Not everyone has these things.

Kristin Larsen, six-figure blogger and founder of Believe in a Budget, knows the importance of accepting responsibility. Here's what she told me:

> I've always had the positive attitude that if I put in a lot of prep work and sweat equity, then my efforts would pay off down the road. When I started my blog, I had no idea when "down the road" would happen. But there have been dozens of "down the road" instances in which blogging has paid off. It's completely changed my life and even the lives of those around me.

The lesson is simple. Don't let a bad situation that you can't control spoil your day. You—and you alone—are responsible for the outcomes in your business and life.

LEAN INTO THE FEAR

When fear bubbles up, practice leaning into the fear. One way to do this is to take baby steps outside your comfort zone.

Cat Le Blanc, business strategist for online-based entrepreneurs, describes how she overcame her fear of appearing on camera:

> It took me a long time to realize just how much I was blocking myself. I have been on a huge personal growth journey in creating and growing this business. In the beginning I couldn't even go on camera. I got over this by stretching my comfort zone little by little using baby steps. I first made super short videos for my clients as these were people who already liked me. Then I got myself a teleprompter so I wouldn't have to remember my lines. Eventually I got so comfortable I didn't need it. With everything that seems challenging or even impossible, I take baby steps until one day I can do it.

The fear never goes away. Learn how to do it scared and, like Cat, you can achieve anything.

CONNECT TO YOUR WHY

When pursuing a big goal, one of the most powerful tools you can master is to connect with your why. This is the reason you're pursuing your goal.

In chapter one we talked about setting *meaningful* goals. You thought about why you want to have a successful blog and who you want to help. Now, you need to set an intention to remain connected to these reasons.

The bigger your goal, the deeper your reasons for blogging need to be. When Lena Gott, blogger at WhatMommyDoes.com, achieved her first $10,000 in one month she realized that money was no longer enough of a motivator. Here's what she told me:

> I finally realized that money on its own is not a good motivator for me. I need something bigger to keep me motivated to continue my business. I like setting goals and beating them, but growing my

> *business just to have more money? That wasn't enough. I needed to get over my motivational block.*
>
> *That's when I decided to start teaching other moms how to do what I've done—build a blog that supports their families. I started a site called Adventures in Blogging where I document my journey and share lessons learned from running my own blog.*
>
> *To date, I've had over 8,000 students come through and many of my students went from struggling blogger to being able to pay all of their bills, including their mortgages, with their newfound success. This is my new why!*

Here're the steps to help you identify and leverage your biggest reason(s) for blogging. Start by visualizing your big goal. Then ask yourself the following questions:

1. Why is this goal important to me?
2. What is at stake if I don't reach my goal?
3. How will my life change when I achieve my goal?
4. How will the world (or some part of it) change when I achieve my goal?

In your favorite journal or in the Blogger Habits Workbook (which you can download at BloggerHabits.com) record your motivations. Write down everything that comes to mind. You can always discard ideas later.

Now, prioritize your motivations in order of most important to least. Which ones move you the most? Which do you connect with emotionally? Rewrite your motivations in order from highest to lowest. Discard any that you don't connect deeply with.

Next, place your list somewhere you'll see every day—stick a post-it note on your computer, hang it on the wall, set a notification on your phone. Finally, set an intention to review your motivations every day. For example, you could review them each morning when you first wake up.

When you read your motivations, take a few moments to close your eyes and visualize yourself as if you've already achieved your goal. Think about how your life will be, including how it will impact the people you love and the audience you serve. Remember how the connection makes you feel.

Also, make sure you review your list of motivations every time fear or doubt threaten to surface. This will help you keep moving when you're feeling overwhelmed or want to give up.

WRITE AFFIRMATION(S)

Don't be put off by the word affirmation. An affirmation is simply a mantra you repeat to reprogram your brain. This may seem woo-woo, but stick with me here. Affirmations really can work.

Two types of affirmations help with habit three. The first type reverses a negative story you tell yourself. For example, I used to think I'd be betraying my family if I invested too much time in my blog. My number one role is mom and wife and I was scared that my business would take away from that.

Once I recognized this fear was holding me back, I created an affirmation:

> *I'm effortlessly managing a six-figure business while enjoying quality time with my family.*

This affirmation turns my fear of losing time with my family into a positive belief (lots of quality family time). Don't copy my affirmation word for word. The key to an effective affirmation is making it personal to you.

The second type of affirmation states your goal as if it has already happened. Here's one of mine:

> *I'm so happy and grateful that I have now sold over 100,000 books and helped thousands of people stay home doing work they love.*

This affirmation reflects my main goal to sell 100,000 books. It works because it focuses my mind on the positive outcome I am working toward.

As with motivations, remember to repeat your affirmations every day. Also visualize how your life will look and how you will feel when your affirmation is real.

CREATE A VISION BOARD

Vision boards are yet another way to visualize how your life will improve when you achieve your goal. There's no one way to create a vision board. The idea is to collect images that reflect your big goal. Your vision board should be personal to you. You want to *feel* what it will be like when you achieve your dreams.

Some people create a physical board and hang it on the wall. Others create a secret Pinterest board and pin images to it. I prefer to change the screensaver on my laptop to reflect my latest goal. If you're a visual person, try creating your own version of a vision board. Get creative, have fun, and see what works for you.

FIND A STATE OF FLOW

The previous strategies are designed to reprogram your brain. Once you fix your sights on a goal and think about it daily, you become aware of new opportunities. You're also in the right frame of mind to act on these opportunities.

But sometimes you can focus too much on a goal. If you're busy fixating on the outcome, how much do you enjoy the process of getting there? And once you reach your goal, how long does your sense of achievement last? A day? Maybe a week?

According to research, goal setting can lead to unethical behavior, a narrowed focus, distorted risks, and reduced intrinsic motivation. The next few strategies combat this effect. They should be used in conjunction with one or more of the previous tools.

> *These tools will help you avoid burnout and enjoy the process of building your blog.*

The first tool is finding flow. Think about a time when you became so involved in what you were doing that the rest of the world seemed to disappear. Perhaps you were practicing a skill or learning something new. Time passed without you noticing.

Psychologists call this "flow." There's a TED talk by Mihaly Csikszentmihalyi which discusses how flow is the secret to happiness. The surprising thing is, not only does this practice lead to more happiness, you also experience greater success and less stress.

To find flow, take whatever project or task you're working on and concentrate solely on the current activity. Savor the moment, the joy of creating something new, the excitement of embarking on a project, the pleasure that comes from doing a task well. See how long you can lose yourself in what you're doing.

The more you practice this the better you'll master the technique. You'll also begin to identify the tasks that come most naturally to you. These are the activities that are within your zone of genius—the things you want to spend the most time doing.

MEDITATE

Meditation is another powerful tool with many uses. It can help you stay present, overcome fears, deal with stress, and much more. One randomized trial examined the effects of mediation on 90 cancer patients. The seven-week program reduced symptoms of stress in the patients by 31 percent.

If you're new to meditation, start with a guided meditation. I like the Head Space app. You can try it for free and if you decide to keep the app, the annual fee is reasonable. The full app offers hundreds of meditations for everything from stress to sleep.

Many people incorporate a short meditation into their morning routine. Meditating for as little as five or 10 minutes a day can lead to improved health and happiness. So, you have nothing to lose by giving it a try.

PRACTICE GRATITUDE

If you're struggling to find flow and are skeptical about mediation, then this next habit may be the answer for you. It takes just a few minutes each day and requires no special skills. I'm talking about recognizing the things for which you're most thankful. These may be small, such as a kind word or deed from a stranger, or big, such as your children's health and happiness.

As well as making you happier, you may also discover that you'll get more of these things in your life as a result. Try being thankful for a small financial gift. You may be surprised to find more money flowing your way.

For the greatest impact, make gratitude a daily habit. For example, share the things you're thankful for at family dinner, or keep a daily gratitude journal. Since starting my gratitude journal (over a year ago) my mood has improved. I find it easier to focus on the good in my life.

> *Gratitude is about spending more time enjoying what you already have and less time worrying about what you may be missing out on.*

CREATE BOUNDARIES

One of the biggest struggles for people who work online is making time for other areas of life, such as family, self-care, and community. It's easy to work long hours and neglect your health and relationships.

Successful people know that they can build a business *and* create a life they love. One of my favorite work–life balance tools is setting boundaries. Personal boundaries free you from guilt and people-pleasing. They provide clarity for you and those you love.

> *"Compassionate people ask for what they need. They say no when they need to, and when they say yes, they mean it. They're compassionate because their boundaries keep them out of resentment." — Brené Brown, Rising Strong*

If you want to create boundaries in your life, start by thinking about where you need a boundary. For example, if you work at an office, do you need to leave work at a set time each day? If you're neglecting your health, do you need to dedicate time to exercise? Decide on what boundary will eliminate the biggest source of conflict or guilt in your life.

Next, set expectations by telling the people who are impacted by your boundary. Then, leverage habit two and create systems to help you keep to your boundary. For example, I stop work at three p.m. each day and lock my laptop in our office. Removing access to my computer reduces the temptation to work. Out of sight is out of mind.

Miranda Nahmias, six-figure blogger at MirandaNahmias.com, said this about boundaries:

> *In the last year, I've been working on my time management skills. Making small changes to how I run my business day-to-day has made it easier to get everything done and I feel less like I am running on a hamster wheel. One of the biggest changes I've made is setting a rule where I stop working for the night at eight p.m., and I no longer work Sundays. This has allowed me to get in some crucial self-care and family time that I was really missing out on.*

SURROUND YOURSELF WITH POSITIVE PEOPLE

If you only adopt one strategy from habit three, then make it this one. People who believe in you and your goals lift you up. You feel supported and are more likely to pursue new opportunities. In contrast, negative people bring you down. They remind you of what's bad about your life and feed into your fears and self-doubts.

> *Avoid toxic people and surround yourself with supporters.*

Many bloggers interviewed for this book participate in a mastermind. We talked about masterminds in chapter eight. You can also join online communities—just avoid any groups in which people complain and participate in negative talk. If your budget allows, consider hiring a coach or mentor.

These are just a handful of ways to master habit three and improve your mindset. There are many more. Allie Bjerk, success coach and digital strategist, describes another simple strategy:

> *There's this concept called resistance that often comes up for those growing a business. Resistance comes in forms of procrastination, self-doubt, and imposter syndrome. But sometimes, if you take action fast enough, you can outrun the resistance and start building up your confidence instead.*

Habit three is a lifelong practice. There's always more you can do to improve your mindset and achieve even bigger goals. The question is—how much do you want it?

ACTION STEPS

1. Read through and pick one or more of these tools to help you focus on your big goal:
> Give Up the Blame Game
> Connect to Your Why
> Write Affirmations

> Create a Vision Board

2. Now, pick one or more of these tools to help you balance your life and enjoy the process of building your blog:

> Find a State of Flow

> Meditate

> Practice Gratitude

> Create Boundaries

> Surround Yourself With Positive People

3. Practice each tool for at least a month. Be prepared to experiment and never stop working on yourself. You are your own greatest obstacle, but you can also get out of your own way.

Now, read the final chapters and see how these successful bloggers are working on habit three. Note how each person recognizes the importance of self-belief and has a positive mindset. We all struggle with fear and self-doubt. When you read these stories, you'll discover that you're not alone. You can do this. You can create a six-figure blog and a life you love.

CHAPTER 15: NINA GARCIA

Even now, each time I shift my mindset, I not only stretch myself beyond my comfort zone and grow as a person, I also grow the business.

Nina Garcia is a mom of three boys, including twins, and the blogger behind Sleeping Should Be Easy, a go-to parenting blog and resource for moms of young kids. Her passion is helping overwhelmed moms enjoy parenthood. Nina writes about discipline, behavior, how kids learn, family life, raising twins, and being a working mom.

What is your favorite business book and why?

I just read two fantastic books. *Go-Givers Sell More*, by Bob Burg and John David Mann, is about creating value for our readers and customers. The second one, *Dollars Flow to Me Easily* by Richard Dotts, isn't exactly a business book, but it talks about why we need to stop negative thoughts of fear, worry, and anxiety, and how doing so allows us to receive the abundance we want in life.

How long did it take from starting your blog/online business until you were consistently earning $8,000 per month or more?

I started the blog as a hobby. Like many moms, I recorded snippets about motherhood, from lessons I was learning to useful tips I wanted to refer to down the line.

This went on for about two years until I decided I'd make my blog public so others could see what I was writing. I then signed up for Amazon's affiliate program and added Google AdWords on the blog, where, three years later, I was earning about $10 a month.

Only later did it finally dawn on me that I might be able to make more than a few bucks a month from blogging. I kept hearing about other bloggers making a full-time living from what they do. I wasn't trying to quit my job and just wanted some extra income—$200 per month was my "dream" goal. I also thought it would take me forever to get there, especially after years of only making $10 per month. But guess what: the following month after setting that goal, I made $197.52.

That was the start of treating the blog as an income-producing activity, and not only a hobby. Once I decided to take it seriously, it took two and a half years to hit that $8,000 per month mark, and it's continued to grow from there.

Blogging truly is amazing. It has allowed me to earn more money than I ever did in the past, while also working fewer hours.

> **What single strategy or habit had the biggest impact on your business when going from zero to $100,000?**

Changing my mindset.

Most of us believe we're simply who we are and tell ourselves stories about what's possible for us and what's not.

For instance, it would never have occurred to me to make a full-time income from blogging had someone not planted that seed in my head. I saw myself as having a regular job for the rest of my life. Only when I changed my mindset from the blog as a side hustle to earning full-time wages did this change actually happen.

I wasn't in the clear just yet, though. Because even once I realized I could earn enough from the blog to quit my job, I still didn't adopt the mindset of a business owner. I treated myself as a freelancer, someone who, at the end of the day, has a job but doesn't own a business. I didn't set my sights on becoming a business owner, thinking I didn't have it in me. I even convinced myself that I was just fine in my comfort zone, that I didn't want to go bigger.

The trouble is, for five months after having left my job to blog full-time, I was earning the same amount as I had been when I was working on the blog on the side! It wasn't until I shifted my mindset and defined my identity as a business owner that the income finally began to rise.

Even now, each time I shift my mindset, I not only stretch myself beyond my comfort zone and grow as a person, I also grow the business.

What new habit or routine has most improved your life in the last year?

Being happy and reminding myself that everything always works out.

My first several months as a full-time blogger were filled with fear, anxiety, and worry. I anticipated things that never actually happened ("What if I run out of money?") because I wanted to beat disappointment to the punch. I figured that if I anticipated bad things happening, that at least I "saw it coming" and wouldn't feel as disappointed. I was trying to protect myself with these negative thoughts, and even assumed I was being practical and realistic for doing so.

But then I found this amazing quote: "You are where your attention is." Focusing on being broke, anxious, and worried is going to keep you broke, anxious, and worried. But shifting attention to joy, abundance, and success—even when all evidence says otherwise—only brings more joy, abundance, and success.

If I had continued working from my circumstances ("I don't earn enough to hire anyone," "I need to save every penny because I'm not making much"), then I would've remained stuck in my circumstances. Worrying and being afraid won't get me anywhere. Now when I feel those emotions, I shift my thinking from worry and fear to joy and gratitude.

When did you hire your first virtual assistant or other help? What advice would you give new bloggers regarding outsourcing?

The first person I hired on a regular basis was a tech person (I still use his services). At that point, I was in the first stages of blogging full-time and resisted the idea of hiring someone on a recurring monthly basis. I was still very much in the "do it yourself to save money" mentality.

But blessings come in disguises, and I had received a notice about a potential malware attack on my blog. And if there's one thing that scares me to pieces, it's dealing with tech stuff. I've had enough experiences with tweaking some piece of code only to mess up the entire website, so I know this is not my forte. When I got the malware notice, I knew I needed to hire someone to handle this for me, someone who knew more than I did about tech stuff, had the skills and resources to protect the site, and the knowledge to fix errors. And I'm so glad I did!

That one monthly expense has given me a huge return, like faster site speed, more reliable hosting, time saved from little tweaks, and peace of mind. And that goes beyond tech stuff and applies to other outsourcing and hiring I now do. These days, I don't see hiring strictly as an expense, but as an investment that flows right back to the business.

As a new blogger, it's common to do as much as you can yourself, especially since you likely have more time than money to get things done. But don't let that hold you back from outsourcing. You don't have to spend hundreds or thousands of dollars to hire help.

For instance, you can set aside a percentage of the money you make for tasks you either can't or don't want to do. Then, use that newfound time to do other tasks that are going to grow your business and eventually provide a return on your investment. Maybe you can use that time to focus on SEO, which would bring in more traffic and ad income, or create a digital product that will earn you passive income once it's finished.

As your business grows, you can increase how much you spend on hiring, but don't assume that just because you're not earning a lot that you can't outsource yet. Your time is free, but also limited. Invest in your blog, knowing you'll get the money back in other ways.

> *What would you do differently if you were to start a new blog/online business today (and couldn't leverage your existing audience)?*

I would start with a business in mind and a picture of what I wanted it to look like down the line. I'd have a clear definition of who the blog serves and narrow down not just the niche, but also what sets it apart from other blogs in the same category.

These days, we simply have too many options and resources. Businesses can't just blend in.

> *Looking back now, what is something you worried about/spent too much time doing that wasn't important down the road?*

I don't know if there was one specific task, but there was a combination of tasks that didn't even make a dent in how much money I made or the impact I was able to have. Things like wasting time tweaking code, or following a zillion people on social media hoping they'd follow me back.

This isn't to say I don't do these tasks and tweaks, but I make sure they're actually contributing to something meaningful.

> *What was the biggest obstacle you faced in building your business to where it is today? How did you overcome it?*

I used to think of having to move beyond my comfort zone as an obstacle, but now I look at it as an opportunity to grow. It feels safe and familiar to stay within my comfort zone, but doing so keeps me from expanding the business and learning more about myself.

Whenever I feel myself getting anxious or scared, I don't pile the excuses anymore or run the other way. Instead, I ask myself if this could be a good opportunity. If so, I commit to getting it done, even if I'm still uncomfortable with it, and only later will I feel confident about it. But it starts with making that commitment to just do it, despite initial fears.

What's your advice for bloggers who are still struggling?

Work from a place of serving your readers. I still follow this advice, and always will, because it reminds me of why I do what I do and gives me the most joy. Truly understand your readers, treat them with respect, go above and beyond, and show excellence in everything you do for them. Be grateful that you have an audience to serve, whether you have 10 readers or 10 million.

Serve your readers, and the money will follow.

These days, I measure success by how much of a positive impact I'm able to make in someone's life. Yes, I still watch the numbers, but when I get emails from readers thanking me for what I do, that's when I know my actions are aligning with my purpose.

How can readers connect with you?

A fantastic way to connect with me is through my weekly newsletters, which readers tell me they LOVE. For instance, I just got an email from a reader who had this to say about them:

"I cannot believe how many stories of yours ring a bell, as if this is my life you're specifically talking about. Thank you for all your newsletters. I inhale every single one of them. Keep up the good work."

Plus, you'll also get my ebook, *Time Management Strategies for the Overwhelmed Mom*, when you sign up (at no cost to you): sleepingshouldbeeasy.com/list

CHAPTER 16: ALLIE BJERK

*Once I realized that I was enough and that I knew
all I needed to know to be successful, everything
changed.*

Allie Bjerk is a success and business coach and digital strategist. She helps online entrepreneurs create more intentional lives.

What is your favorite business book and why?

When it comes to reading for business, it's hard to choose just one favorite book. Some books that have resonated over the years include *Expert Secrets* by Russell Brunson, *How to Win Friends and Influence People* by Dale Carnegie (though that's more of a life skills book), and Jordan B. Peterson's *12 Rules for Life*. I've found that so many books in the personal development space apply not only to our lives, but our businesses as well.

How long did it take from starting your blog/online business until you were consistently earning $8,000 per month or more?

It took me roughly five years in business to consistently earn $8,000-plus per month. For a long time, I was stuck at the $3,500 mark, and that wasn't profit. For about five years, I was profiting roughly $14,000 per year, after all of the coaching and courses I was investing in. But then, something clicked.

I stopped looking to all sorts of different experts and courses to tell me how to manage and grow my businesses. Once I realized that I was enough and that I knew all I needed to know to be successful, everything changed.

What new habit or routine has most improved your life in the last year?

The biggest routine that has improved my life in the last year is focusing on being really intentional with how I spend my time. I'm a mother of three young children and running a six-figure business from my laptop, so for my own sanity, I've simplified everything. I've simplified my business offerings, the emails I'm subscribed to, and the content I consume. I have *one* business mentor that I follow and I'm sticking with one strategy. I'm no longer throwing spaghetti at the wall in hopes that it will stick. I chose *one* type of service to offer and one type of client. Now, I'm laser-focused on becoming one of the best in the industry.

Looking back now, what is something you worried about/spent too much time doing that wasn't important down the road?

When I look back on my years in business, I spent too much time working with the wrong clients. I was scared that if I niched down, I would never get another client again. Dramatic, I know, but it's scary to think of telling someone who wants to pay you that you don't want their money, right? In hindsight, I wish I had chosen an ideal client much sooner and stuck with it.

I also spent a lot of time obsessing over the decisions I was making in my business. I was in a constant state of "what's next, what's next?" I was constantly coming up with new ideas and promotions, instead of just optimizing the ones that I had. One year, I looked at my tax return and realized that I had profited $14,000.

Fourteen thousand dollars for three hundred and sixty-five days of obsession.

It felt so wrong. I remember thinking, "I could have worked at the local fast food restaurant and brought home more money, while having zero stress."

The thing that made me most upset wasn't the dollar amount, it was the amount of pressure I had placed on myself. I equated high amounts of job stress with high amounts of income. With the balance of income to stress feeling so off kilter, I only had one choice. Lower the stress. Which, coincidentally, increased the income. Funny how that works.

Having more fun in your business brings on those higher pay days. When you're enjoying what you do, your audience can feel it. It inspires them and builds the trust needed for stronger reader and client relationships.

> *What would you do differently if you were to start a new blog/online business today (and couldn't leverage your existing audience)?*

If I were to start again at zero, I would give myself permission to have fun with it from the beginning. I would trust that I knew enough to start with what I have and that taking action always trumps the best laid plans. I would fail fast and improve faster. I'd pick an idea (yes, just one) and run with it as far and as fast as I could.

There's this concept called resistance that often comes up for those growing a business. Resistance comes in forms of procrastination, self-doubt, and imposter syndrome. But sometimes, if you take action fast enough, you can outrun the resistance and start building up your confidence instead.

> *What was the biggest obstacle you faced in building your business to where it is today? How did you overcome it?*

The largest obstacle I faced in my business was myself.

I grew up extroverted and thus, I thought, super-ultra-confident in all areas of my life.

However, learning how to run a business can open your eyes to parts of yourself that you didn't know were there. Or, better yet, help you realize why those traits and habits exist in the first place, and how they could be holding you back.

For example, my entire life, I thought I worked best under pressure.

In college, I was notorious for waiting until the night before a test or a project was due and then cramming it all in by staying up all night (thanks to lots of sugar-free Red Bulls and extra-shot lattes). I always finished the projects.

But if I got a B instead of an A? "Well, that's just because I pulled an all-nighter to get it done. If I had started sooner, I definitely would have gotten an A."

Turns out I had a fear of failure and liked to give myself an easy excuse as to why I didn't get the best grade possible.

When it came to being a business owner and managing client projects, this fear of failure kept showing up in different ways. Sometimes it looked like not finishing projects or a lack of responding to client emails—not cool.

My mind and my fear of failure was becoming a self-fulfilling prophecy.

Once I realized there was a connection between my all-nighters in college and the fact that I wasn't giving my current work projects all my focus, it changed the game for me.

I realized that my value as a human was not directly correlated to my clients' results.

With this new self-awareness, I was able to do the work to start pushing that fear of failure aside. "The work" being journaling, working with a mindset coach, and taking baby steps toward proving to myself that I will do what I say I will do, no matter what.

My confidence in myself and my ability to make smart decisions and run an intentional business has soared. And my income levels have followed.

If you're struggling with confidence in yourself or going through a bout of imposter syndrome, start by getting really good at something small. "I always keep my inbox at zero," or even, "I floss my teeth every day." These baby steps lead to increased self-trust and knowing that even when it's a big scary decision or opportunity, you won't let yourself down.

What's your advice for bloggers who are still struggling?

My advice for bloggers and online business owners who are struggling would be to first identify who you really want to serve and then become the best you can be at doing just that. Also, trust the process. When you reflect on your journey, you'll see that every step you've taken so far has become a building block in the foundation of your business.

Sometimes we can feel impatient or frustrated if we aren't where we want to be in business. In those times, it's important to stay focused and grateful for the present. Taking one baby step toward your goal is better than staying still.

And if you're struggling to even know what that one baby step is, first identify your goal.

What exactly do you want? What's the very next thing you want? Once you've identified the goal, figure out what the problem is that's keeping you from reaching the goal. Every problem is made up of obstacles. Once you understand which obstacles are in front of you, you can map out the steps necessary to overcome those obstacles and reach your goals.

Following this framework has changed the way I map out my to-do lists and has helped me gain a ton of insight into where I get tripped up. Once you start understanding your own resistance and overcoming those challenges, there's no limit to the momentum you'll feel when you're taking action and busting through those obstacles.

You've got this!

How can readers connect with you?

If you'd like to receive more content, you can visit my website at ProsperityLab.com. You can also connect with me on Instagram and Facebook.

CHAPTER 17: KRISTIN LARSEN

One of my favorite things about online business is the potential income increase in a relatively short amount of time compared to a traditional job.

Kristin Larsen is the founder of Believe in a Budget, a blog that helps others learn how to side hustle, save money, and budget. In addition, Kristin teaches entrepreneurs how to start an online business and become a Pinterest virtual assistant.

What is your favorite business book and why?

My favorite business book is *Studio: Creative Spaces for Creative People*. I'm a visual person, and this book speaks my love language. It's full of home offices and creative spaces from all types of businesses all over the world.

Every time I flip through this book, I love reading about the different spaces and types of jobs these entrepreneurs have. Everyone is so unique!

Although I might be in a different line of work than most people in the book, I can relate to wanting a positive workplace that brings joy and comfort. It's motivating to see people in their work environment, and it makes me want to have the best possible work space for myself.

How long did it take from starting your blog/online business until you were consistently earning $8,000 per month or more?

When I first started my blog, there was a lot of sweat equity involved. Although I was working hard, I didn't make any income in the beginning.

On month four, I finally published my first income report, which was around $60. It was the best paycheck I had ever received, and I was so excited to share this with my readers. This gave me an extra boost of confidence to keep going and work harder.

As I continued to track my earnings and publish income reports, it was amazing to watch my numbers grow. Every few months I would see my income level bump up. I soon hit my first milestone, which was $1,000. Shortly after, my monthly income rose again to around $5,000.

About 18 months after launching Believe in a Budget, I crossed the $8,000 per month mark. I was super excited. This meant I was inching closer to the next big milestone, which was five figures per month.

One of my favorite things about online business is the potential income increase in a relatively short amount of time compared to a traditional job. For example, in my first year of blogging, I made around $13,000 on the side. Much of my first year was devoted to putting in time, effort, and learning.

I also saved as much money as possible during that year because I wanted to leave my day job and blog full-time. I re-examined my budget and my spending habits, and managed to put away six months of living expenses. Fortunately, when I left my day job, my blog was bringing in so much income that I didn't have to dip into my savings.

In my second year of blogging, which also happened to be my first full year of being self-employed, I made around $91,000. In my third year, I earned just under $290,000.

There is no way this kind of growth would have been possible at my day job. While I enjoyed my line of work, I had reached my salary cap.

Although I was comfortable with my salary, my mentality with money was either spend less or find a second job and earn more. That's why starting my blog as a side hustle with the intention of turning it into my full-time job was such a big goal for me.

What single strategy or habit had the biggest impact on your business when going from zero to $100,000?

The best habit I've maintained is continuing education. Regardless of where I am with my blog and business, I'm always striving to learn more.

As a new blogger, I couldn't read enough about blogging. I wanted to learn how everything worked, whether it was installing a theme on my website, publishing a blog post, or sending out an email to my readers.

Over time, I started to focus on one area at a time. It was important for me to have basic knowledge of a subject, even if I knew it wasn't my area of expertise. This way if I were to outsource that part of my business, I would know exactly what I needed help with, as well as the goal I wanted to achieve.

As Believe in a Budget started to grow, my blog became a launching pad for so many new things. Within my first years as a blogger, I released my first ebook about side hustling.

In my second and third years of blogging, things really started happening! I launched two courses and created multiple digital products, all geared around side hustling and Pinterest—two very different things.

In addition to creating these products, I had to learn how to promote them. The amount of work that went into creating and marketing was astronomical. I spent a lot of time behind the scenes. This included purchasing a couple of courses, doing all the homework, and applying what I was learning.

I also joined a couple of mastermind groups. And I had accountability partners to help me stay on task.

I think one of the biggest mistakes I could have made is pretending to know everything and not seeking help. This would have stunted the growth of my business and placed limitations on my areas of expertise.

What new habit or routine has most improved your life in the last year?

The best—and the hardest—habit that has improved the quality of my life is creating my best version of a work-life balance.

For most of my first year blogging, I had a full-time day job. When I wasn't at work, I would get up early, work late into the evening and spend my weekends learning about blogging.

I was determined to succeed, and nothing was going to stop my goal of quitting my day job to become a full-time blogger. Fortunately, my hard work paid off and I was able to give notice at work within ten months of launching Believe in a Budget.

Fast forward to my third year of blogging, and I was struggling mentally. I felt the urge to work all the time. I had the mentality that if I didn't work, I'd be losing out on making money online.

Finally, something had to give. I was burning out and losing steam. I took a long hard look at my business and realized it was time to make a change.

My goal now is to mimic a typical work week I had in the past. I take weekends off and most weekday evenings. Occasionally, this rule gets broken, for example if I'm working on a big project and need to check in with members of my team.

This new routine has improved the quality of my life. I look forward to weekends and spending time away from the computer. My anxiety and stress levels have decreased. I don't feel burned out, and I look forward to starting the work week on Mondays.

I also have more freedom and flexibility and I'm much more organized, focused, and productive. This allows me to be fully available to family, friends, and living my life outside of work hours.

> **When did you hire your first virtual assistant or other help? What advice would you give new bloggers regarding outsourcing?**

Hiring and working with virtual assistants has been such a game changer for my business.

In the early days of blogging, I was on a tight budget. Essentially, there was no budget (hence the name Believe in a Budget!). I was a DIY extraordinaire and determined to learn how to do everything myself.

Well, this only got me so far. I quickly learned that my lack of expertise was slowing down my business. While I was trying to save money, I was wasting time. I realized that to move forward and focus on what I was good at, I needed to hire help.

The first virtual assistant I hired was for a small, one-time job. I had just purchased a paid theme and didn't understand how to import the theme and set everything up.

What had been taking me a few days to figure out, with no progress and pure frustration on my part, was solved in one hour with a small payment to a website designer. I was in total awe!

Since then, I've worked with a variety of virtual assistants in different capacities. Though, even as my income has grown, I'm still budget conscious. I weigh the pros and cons of hiring a virtual assistant and how the outcome will impact my brand.

In the beginning, I worked with virtual assistants who were just starting out online. This worked out well. I got help from a VA who knew more about a specific area than me and was ready to work hard. The VA benefited because they were able to get more experience working with clients.

Early on, I worried that I would have to hire someone for ongoing work. When I realized that I could hire someone for a one-time project, it eliminated the financial pressure I had placed on myself. Being able to hire a virtual assistant as needed, at a price point I was comfortable with, helped me grow my blog.

Whether someone is a new blogger or an experienced pro, one of the perks of working with a virtual assistant is the ability to hire based on experience and pay scale.

> *What would you do differently if you were to start a new blog/online business today (and couldn't leverage your existing audience)?*

If I were to start again today, the first thing I would do after setting up my website would be to focus on growing my email list. This was an area I overlooked in my first year of blogging. I didn't understand the importance of having subscribers and what to do with them once they were on my list.

After a lot of research, things started to make sense! Using an email list, I could contact my readers and let them know when a new blog post was published, if I had a new freebie, or I could promote an ebook or product.

Prior to this I communicated with my audience by responding to blog comments (I still personally respond to every comment I receive on my blog). But I regret not setting up an email opt-in sooner. If someone takes the time to leave a comment, they will most likely sign up for your email list.

Fortunately, I've made up for lost time! I've spent a lot of time learning about my email provider and have developed a strong relationship with my newsletter audience.

> *Looking back now, what is something you worried about/spent too much time doing that wasn't important down the road?*

When I first started my blog, I spent way too much time reviewing analytics and data. I would gauge my success by checking how many people followed me on social media per day and I got upset if I noticed someone had unfollowed me. Yes, my social media stats were small enough, so I could determine this.

I would check my analytics to see how many people visited my site the previous day, as well as log into Google Adsense to see if my ads had earned any money. I think on a good day, I made around five cents per day!

Instead of reviewing all these numbers, I should have been more productive. Reviewing my analytics daily, or even weekly, was pretty moot in the early stages of blogging. My time would have been better spent growing my presence on social media instead of checking data.

As my blog gained traction and my traffic increased, that's when analytics started to matter. Once this happened, it was important to learn where my traffic was coming from, which blog posts were performing well, and how long readers were staying on my website.

While I think analytics and data are important for a website, they really aren't useful in the beginning stages of blogging!

> **What was the biggest obstacle you faced in building your business to where it is today? How did you overcome it?**

The biggest obstacle I faced had nothing to do with building my business—it had to do with myself.

In general, I'm a private person. I wasn't comfortable sharing my blog with people who knew me. I don't use social media outside of my business and wasn't ready to have my real life crossover online.

As a new blogger, I didn't share a headshot of myself and only used my first name. As my blog grew and I was presented with new opportunities, I had a decision to make. Do I remain anonymous and in my comfort zone, or do I take down my barriers and use my full name and headshot?

While it seemed like a no-brainer to go for it, I made a list of what I was comfortable with sharing online once I revealed my identity. I reviewed my previously published blog posts and removed anything I didn't feel comfortable becoming common knowledge.

The other obstacle I encountered was sharing my blog with family and friends. When I started my blog, I didn't tell anyone. I have always disliked attention of any kind, whether it's positive or negative.

Even though I treated my blog like a business, it felt like a personal part of me was exposed online. This got even harder as I started sharing my online income reports. It's something I still struggle with today.

While part of me knows that my income reports inspire and motivate others, and I'm always humbled by kind words from readers, I worry that I'm being judged for sharing this type of information.

Fortunately, as time went by, I became more comfortable discussing my blog and online business with family and friends. Having their support has meant the world to me and I'm grateful for their encouragement.

> **What's your advice for bloggers who are still struggling?**

Blogging can be challenging at any level, but the hardest part for me was starting out. However, I never felt like giving up and always had a hustle mentality that if I worked hard, my efforts would pay off.

I went into blogging wanting to earn an income and quit my day job. I was on a mission to create a blog that would help and inspire other people, as well as provide an honest income for myself.

For the first year, I spent every waking moment working on my blog. After four months of blogging, I earned my first $60 paycheck. But that wasn't going to pay the bills!

Then I realized that I was measuring the wrong things. My results were so much more than the amount of money earned. So, I focused on other accomplishments as a beginner blogger.

For example, I had established a writing schedule and was publishing three blog posts per week. I had gained authority in my niche and developed stronger writing skills. Readers were responding to my blog posts and leaving comments. I was creating a strong marketing strategy on Pinterest, which would later allow me to market myself as a Pinterest expert. I was also starting to make friends online, many of whom I've now met in person and am friends with in real life.

To this day, if I feel like I'm in a slump or struggling, I make a list of all the great things happening. It's so easy to overlook the positives and focus solely on the negative. This kind of attitude helps me stay motivated and clear my head.

I've always had the positive attitude that if put in a lot of prep work and sweat equity, then my efforts will pay off down the road. When I started my blog, I had no idea when "down the road" would happen. But there have been dozens of "down the road" instances during which blogging has paid off. It's completely changed my life and even the lives of those around me.

How can readers connect with you?

Readers can find out more at my website, BelieveInABudget.com. You can also connect with me on Facebook, Twitter, Instagram, and Pinterest.

CHAPTER 18: LENA GOTT

Getting over the fear of failure is the biggest thing any business owner can overcome. Give it your best shot and try to truly help people.

Lena Gott is a CPA turned stay-at-home mom who left the corporate world when her first baby was born. She grew her blog, WhatMommyDoes, over the course of many years while her kids were little. She writes about fun stuff like play dates and making memories with your kids, in addition to more serious topics like budgeting and family finances.

What is your favorite business book and why?

My favorite business book is *Millionaire Maker: Act, Think, and Make Money the Way the Wealthy Do* by Loral Langemeier.

It's not so much a business book, as it is about managing your personal finances like a business.

Her methods are rather aggressive (the CPA in me wouldn't recommend being this aggressive with your money), but it's definitely worth a read. The book makes you look at income through a different lens and will change how you approach blog investments.

How long did it take from starting your blog/online business until you were consistently earning $8,000 per month or more?

I was blogging on WhatMommyDoes for several years before I consistently made $8,000 per month. That was because it took me a while to decide to buckle down and focus on growth. I had several hundred blog posts and very little income when I decided something had to change. I was either going to blow this up or give it up! After I began to really focus, it took about 10 months to get it to the $8,000 mark.

I didn't have a lot of free time (or mental capacity) to devote to blogging when the kids were really little. Once my youngest turned two, I felt like I could handle a bit more and that's when I considered taking blogging seriously. By the time he was three, I was all in.

I needed something more to do and I always say my blog is my fourth child!

What single strategy or habit had the biggest impact on your business when going from zero to $100,000?

The best thing I ever did for my business as I was going from zero to $100,000 per year was start a mailing list.

I was able to earn about $3,000 to $4,000 per month from my blog purely from traffic-based income (advertising and sponsorships), but I received a huge boost for relatively little effort once I implemented email marketing in my business.

What new habit or routine has most improved your life in the last year?

The habit that has most improved my life in the last year has been focusing on gratitude and grace. I gave myself grace over shortcomings and missed goals, and I was overall much happier because of it.

I also practiced expressing gratitude for the important people in my life by making more time for them, which included working in much needed downtime for myself.

I like to have a focus word for each year. Two years ago it was "scale." Although I grew the business, I almost burned out in the process. So, last year my word was "flow." That involved trying my best to take events in my life in stride and not worry about the little things. This has helped me tremendously.

When did you hire your first virtual assistant or other help? What advice would you give new bloggers regarding outsourcing?

I waited way too long to hire my first assistant. I waited until I was absolutely swamped with work, stressing out over my to-do list, and barely meeting deadlines for projects. I hired out of desperation, which I wouldn't recommend.

My best advice to newer bloggers would be to hire out at the first sign of overwhelm. Your blog work shouldn't feel like a burden. That's a sign you should delegate tasks.

I always say, if you have that feeling like you just wish you could clone yourself, you're past the point of needing to hire someone. These days, I try to hire proactively, instead of in reaction to stress.

You'll have to give up some of your profits to hire help, but I promise it's easier (and more profitable in the long run) than having things fall through the cracks because you can't keep up.

> *What would you do differently if you were to start a new blog/online business today (and couldn't leverage your existing audience)?*

If I were starting a new business today and couldn't leverage my existing audience, I would do two things. First, I would start with a product that solves a specific need. It's much easier to build a business around selling a specific product that helps a specific person than to build an audience and then figure out what to sell to them.

Second, once I figured out what my product would be, I'd hire out creation of the basics so I didn't have to spend my own time creating. I'd hire out things like initial website creation, logo design, sales pages, and more. That way, when I start actively working on the business, everything is ready for me to jump right in.

Now I know that spending weeks or months setting everything up myself makes me lose motivation very quickly. I'm not into the technical details.

While my team works on setting up the technical side, I can spend my time creating the product itself.

> *Looking back now, what is something you worried about/spent too much time doing that wasn't important down the road?*

Looking back now on my early days of blogging, I spent way too much time agonizing over whether I was good enough. I agonized over every little thing in my business.

Whether somebody would ever want to read my emails....

Whether somebody would dislike my new post....

Whether anybody would buy my products....

All of this doesn't really matter and only serves to overwhelm and frustrate you as the business owner.

I finally realized some important truths that have changed the way I look at my business.

#1 Fact: I'm not good enough for everybody, but some people love what I have to offer. Some people can't stand my emails (and tell me so), but other people email me to tell me that I changed their lives for the better. It's okay if not everyone in your audience thinks your product is awesome as long as you're helping a lot of people who do think it's awesome.

#1 Truth: Getting over the fear of failure is the biggest thing any business owner can overcome. Give it your best shot and try to truly help people. That's all you can do. Your true fans will stay and everyone else will move on. If you never even start out of fear, you'll sell yourself short.

> *What was the biggest obstacle you faced in building your business to where it is today? How did you overcome it?*

In addition to self-doubt, the biggest obstacle I've faced is staying motivated once I hit a big goal.

When I started my blog, I had a pie-in-the-sky goal of earning $1,000 per month. I would have been happy with earning enough to simply put two kids in preschool at once (which was $395 a month).

When I hit the $1,000 mark, I set what I believed was an insane goal of $10,000 per month. I figured 10 times my pie-in-the-sky goal would be amazing. But when I hit $10,000? It was like I hit my own version of the glass ceiling. I would work just hard enough to get $10,000 each month and once I thought I'd get there by the end of the month, I basically stopped trying.

I really couldn't find my mojo for a while to work any harder than I was.

I finally realized that money on its own is not a good motivator for me.

I need something bigger than that to keep me motivated to continue my business. I like setting goals and beating them, but growing my business just to have more money? That wasn't enough. I needed to get over my motivational block.

That's when I decided to start teaching other moms how to do what I've done— build a blog that supports their families. I started a site called Adventures in Blogging where I document my journey and share lessons learned from running my own blog.

To date, I've had over 8,000 students come through and many of my students went from struggling bloggers to being able to pay all of their bills, including their mortgages, with newfound success. This is my new why!

What's your advice for bloggers who are struggling?

My best advice to anyone who's struggling with their blog is to keep going, be willing to throw out things that don't work, and invest in the business.

Because we don't have a "college of blogging," everyone is out there learning things the hard way. The learning curve is steep, but I promise one day things will just click for you. So many bloggers with amazing potential quit before the point where things "click."

Build on your small wins and make one positive improvement per day.

Also, give yourself permission to drop anything that doesn't work. Every minute you spend doing something useless is a minute you could be spending doing something that generates income.

Most importantly, don't hesitate to invest in education. Many bloggers bootstrap their startup and constantly feel the need to be thrifty.

Business growth and thrift don't often co-exist. You have to make smart investments along the way in tools and resources, especially education.

If you don't know how to do something, you should either learn how to do it or pay someone else to do it. This is how you will keep moving forward.

How can readers connect with you?

Readers can find out more at my website, WhatMommyDoes.com. You can also connect with me on Facebook, Pinterest, Instagram, and Twitter.

CHAPTER 19: CAT LEBLANC

At a core level it was literally getting up every weekday, making the best decisions I could at the time, and doing the work that got me to six figures.

Cat LeBlanc is a business strategist for online-based entrepreneurs. She specializes in helping her clients design, build, and grow a business that is truly unique to them, so they can live life on their terms.

Cat is the host of the podcast Your Business, Your Rules and has written for top publications such as Business Insider and Huffington Post. She is on a mission to help budding online business owners gain independence through entrepreneurship.

What is your favorite business book and why?

I am generally a person who doesn't have one favorite. The book I find myself picking up again and again is *Made to Stick: Why Some Ideas Survive and Others Die* by Chip Heath and Dan Heath.

It's a fascinating insight into human psychology and explains why some untrue ideas perpetuate and why other very important ideas are simply forgotten. I use the concepts to help people understand my ideas and make them more memorable. It always brings me back to understanding how people work.

How long did it take from starting your blog/online business until you were consistently earning $8,000 per month or more?

It took me 18 months to average $8,000 a month. In the beginning stages of my business I was focused on getting paid in full and did not make my payment plans that attractive for clients.

This meant my revenues had big spikes, which was exciting and I loved this, but it meant my revenue had a lot of variance month to month.

Now I focus more on consistent revenue in my business as I have support staff and a different level of expenses.

What single strategy or habit had the biggest impact on your business when going from zero to $100,000?

I was and am very driven to grow my business.

At a core level it involved getting up every weekday, making the best decisions I could at the time, and doing the work that got me to six figures.

There were many times when it seemed like an easier choice to quit and do something else, but I was so committed that it just wasn't an option.

Over time I developed a whole system of chunking down projects from high level strategy to daily actions, a mindset routine, and productivity hacks to ensure I was making the right actions in the right headspace and being productive.

Ultimately it was learning how to manage myself in this way that made the difference. Being a good manager to myself, setting clear action steps, keeping myself feeling good and on track, I was able to harness my commitment into results.

Of course, there is a lot of nuance to that, but what I am saying is that it wasn't a quick fix or magic pill that got me here. It was commitment, work, and self-management.

What new habit or routine has most improved your life in the last year?

The most valuable habit I've been able to develop over the past year is learning to treat this business game a little more lightly.

Business can be a rollercoaster with lots of emotional ups and downs. It's easy to feel strongly about a lot of things because so much is riding on them.

Instead of holding on so tight that every twist and turn is jarring, I'm learning to loosen my grip and enjoy the breeze more.

When did you hire your first virtual assistant or other help? What advice would you give new bloggers regarding outsourcing?

I hired my first help immediately. I made this decision because I believed at the time that otherwise I would not be able to start because I hated writing! I hired help with writing my blog (which I use as a marketing tool rather than my core business model) and with my social media.

Having support in these areas gave me the mental head space to grow the other areas of my business.

> *What would you do differently if you were to start a new blog/online business today (and couldn't leverage your existing audience)?*

If I were starting again, I'd experiment more and be more flexible in the early stages. It does take time to figure out what works. I had a tendency to be fixed on certain ideas in the beginning. If I had the chance to try again, I would pivot more quickly.

I would also get more mindset and health support early on. When you run a business while you have more flexibility and growth potential, you do make more decisions and carry more responsibility. I would prioritize self-care and support from the beginning.

> *Looking back now, what is something you worried about/spent too much time doing that wasn't important down the road?*

I spent a lot of time on my website initially. I spent hours trying to make fancy designs and trying to make different things line up. Now websites are much easier to build than even five years ago, but I definitely wasted a lot of time on small details that made no difference to how many clients I was getting.

> *What was the biggest obstacle you faced in building your business to where it is today? How did you overcome it?*

Honestly, the biggest obstacle in building my business has been me.

Specifically, my fear of being wrong, looking stupid, not having enough expertise, or just messing things up.

I think this is usually the case for most of us. People cite finances or time as the main constraint, but the biggest constraint is almost always in our own heads.

It took me a long time to realize just how much I was blocking myself. I have been on a huge personal growth journey in creating and growing this business. In the beginning I couldn't even go on camera. I got over this by stretching my comfort zone little by little using baby steps. I first made super short videos for my clients as these were people who already liked me. Then I got myself a teleprompter so I wouldn't have to remember my lines. Eventually I got so comfortable I didn't need it. With everything that seems challenging or even impossible, I take baby steps until one day I can do it.

What's your advice for bloggers who are still struggling?

My biggest advice to struggling bloggers is to get help. We grow up in very structured environments. School is incredibly structured. Most career roles are, too. Business is like an open ocean.

Don't leave yourself out there flailing and wondering what to do next. Find someone who has done what you want to do and can guide you.

The truth is no one does this by themselves.

How can readers connect with you?

My website is at CatLeBlanc.com and the Your Business, Your Rules podcast can be found at CatLeBlanc.com/podcast.

CHAPTER 20: MIRANDA NAHMIAS

Success is all about being determined and continuing on when the road gets tough.

Miranda Nahmias is a systematic marketing expert for female online service providers. When she's not writing epic, actionable blog posts, she's doing everything she can to help lady biz bosses achieve their dreams in the most stress-free way possible. Miranda does this by providing amazing resources and done-for-you services that use her proven systematic marketing techniques to allow busy female service providers to score more clients and #growlikewoah in their businesses.

What is your favorite business book and why?

This is an extremely hard question to answer, as I love reading and am constantly checking out new business books. I'm not sure that I could pick one favorite, but a few that were very influential for me included *Profit First* by Mike Michaelowicz, *You Are a Badass at Making Money* by Jen Sincero, and *Expert Secrets* by Russell Brunson.

Profit First showed me how to get my financial systems in place to create a consistently profitable business for myself. *You Are a Badass at Making Money* taught me how to conquer my mindset issues and money blocks. *Expert Secrets* is like a roadmap for visibility and scaling your business that I am constantly turning back to and re-reading.

> *How long did it take from starting your blog/online business until you were consistently earning $8,000 per month or more?*

A little under two years.

> *What single strategy or habit had the biggest impact on your business when going from zero to $100,000?*

Publishing consistent blog content on my website had a huge impact on how successful I've been. Most people find me through Pinterest, which is where I share all of my blog posts. I have relied heavily on content marketing as a big part of my strategy for growing my business, and I think it has significantly helped me grow. The longer I keep publishing high-quality posts, the more of an audience I get.

> *What new habit or routine has most improved your life in the last year?*

In the last year, I've been working on time management skills. Making small changes to how I run my business day-to-day has made it easier to get everything done and I feel less like I'm running on a hamster wheel. One of the biggest changes I've made is setting a rule where I stop working for the night at eight p.m., and I no longer work Sundays. This has allowed me to get in some crucial self-care and family time that I was really missing out on.

> *When did you hire your first virtual assistant or other help? What advice would you give new bloggers regarding outsourcing?*

I hired my first team member about four months after starting my business. Since my business is an agency model, I have pretty much always had help, but mostly they assist with my client work. After about a year and a half in business, I finally hired a few team members that are specifically for helping me, including an online business manager, a bookkeeper, and a virtual assistant.

> *What would you do differently if you were to start a new blog/online business today (and couldn't leverage your existing audience)?*

I would get serious with email marketing right from the start. Originally, I was very hesitant to start an email list, as it seemed really overwhelming. And even when I finally did start my list, I was never consistent about sending them content, even though I had all of my automations and sequences set up. Now that I'm working on scaling my business, I realize how important that list is, and I wish that I'd put more effort into it over the years.

> Looking back now, what is something you worried about/spent too much time doing that wasn't important down the road?

In the beginning, I spent a lot of time trying to sell information products before I had a big list. I wish that I had realized it's almost impossible to sell digital products without a big list, and I wish I had spent more time either growing my list or focusing on getting client work. Now I am in a much better place to sell information products, but I never sold very many of the first few I released.

> What was the biggest obstacle you faced in building your business to where it is today? How did you overcome it?

The biggest obstacle I've faced when building my business has been my introvert personality. When I first started working online, I would've called myself an extreme introvert. I was terrified of interacting with people, and really had to push myself to connect with people online, especially potential clients.

Now, a few years later, I would consider myself more of an introverted extrovert! I still love my down time, and often get exhausted after being on camera all day, but a part of me loves it. It took a long time to get there, but I realized early on that I would need to develop my skills in this area to be successful. So, I constantly pushed myself out of my comfort zone. I forced myself into conversations, interactions, and scenarios that scared me. Eventually I became accustomed to doing things like podcast interviews, discovery calls, and having coffee chats with online friends. Being on camera is second nature to me now!

> What's your advice for bloggers who are still struggling?

Success is all about being determined and keeping going when the road gets tough. It's important to keep persisting and keep working on it. We all have to start somewhere, so try not to compare yourself to others as you work through this process. You will get there eventually, and trust me, it's worth it!

How can readers connect with you?

I'd love to share some of my blog posts with anyone reading this! I publish new content weekly over at MirandaNahmias.com. You can also connect with me on Pinterest and Instagram.

CONCLUSION

A little over nine months ago I embarked on a journey. I set out with an idea for my next book. Along the way I met some amazing people and together we created a blueprint for blogging success.

I couldn't have done this without the help of the 17 bloggers who shared their struggles and triumphs with me. Each person I interviewed provided insight into what it takes to build a six-figure blog. As I immersed myself in their stories—and their businesses—I uncovered two truths.

First, there's no one path to success. We're all unique and there are an infinite number of ways to create a profitable online business. But this is a good thing! It means you can build a business around your strengths and values. A business that fits your life and your ambitions.

Second, there are three habits that *all* successful people practice in some form. They are:

> 1. *Act with purpose: Successful people have a mission and take strategic action to fulfill their vision.*
> 2. *Create systems for success: Successful people create systems so that the essential tasks always get done.*
> 3. *Believe in yourself: Successful people accept responsibility for their results and believe in their power to achieve the desired outcome, no matter what happens.*

Now, it's your turn. This book describes the three habits and how to incorporate them into your blogging life. Read the stories, follow the action steps, and build *your* vision of success.

If you'd like more help, I've created a bonus workbook. This downloadable workbook guides you through the steps to practice the three habits and build your six-figure blog. When you download the workbook, you will get email access to me. I'd love to support you on your journey. It's my mission to help you do work you love. If that sounds like something you want, hop over to the bonus area at BloggerHabits.com

Finally, make sure you visit the bloggers' websites mentioned in this book. Each person featured has built an incredible business and is making a real difference in the world. Learn from those who are already doing what you want to do. And go create your six-figure blog. There's no limit to the wealth and opportunities available to you.

ABOUT SALLY MILLER

Sally is a mom on a mission. She is passionate about answering the question, "Can modern moms have it all?" In a previous life, Sally worked for nineteen years as a project manager and business analyst in London and Silicon Valley. She has a Bachelor's Degree in Computer Science and a Master's Degree in Business Administration.

When her daughter was born, she discovered a new purpose. Sally left her corporate career to be a stay-at-home mom. She wanted to be a full-time mom to her kids. However, she missed the freedom and purpose that came from working. So Sally made a decision: She'd find a way to stay home with her kids and earn an income (without feeling torn between the two).

Sally is a self-confessed research geek and compulsive planner. She loves learning how stuff works, mastering new skills, and sharing her knowledge with others. Since leaving her nine-to-five, Sally has published seven books (and counting). She's also started multiple businesses and is committed to helping others like her earn an income from home.

You can find out more by visiting her website at sallyannmiller.com.

CPSIA information can be obtained
at www.ICGtesting.com
Printed in the USA
LVHW011547210319
611421LV00003B/489/P

9 781719 939393